VEGETABLE GARDENING

THE BEGINNER'S GUIDE WITH STEP-BY-STEP INSTRUCTIONS TO GROWING A KITCHEN GARDEN IN THE BACKYARD WITH PLANTS, FRUITS AND INCREDIBLY DELICIOUS ORGANIC FOODS

KIMBERLEY SMITH

Visit the author's page

Write to: kimb.smith.books@gmail.com

OTHER PUBLICATIONS BY KIMBERLEY SMITH:

Raising Chickens For Eggs:

The Beginner's Guide To Building A Chicken-Coop, To Learn How to Raise A Happy Backyard Flock. A Homesteading Solution While You Are At Home

Hydroponic Gardening:

A Detailed Guide on Hydronics to Learn the Principles Behind Gardening and Build a Wonderful System While at Home. Techniques for Your Vegetable Cultivations

TABLE OF CONTENTS

AUTHOR'S NOTE

Growing your vegetable garden is an enjoyable and beneficial hobby that anyone can shine at.

Home gardening alleviates strain and allows you to be outside in the sunlight.

Vegetable gardening is known to reduce blood pressure and clear the brain. Additionally, the action of nurturing plants and watch them grow produces soothing effects.

If you're curious and eager to have a brand new garden of your own, flourishing with your favorite vegetables in the backyard, you need to follow the steps discussed in this book in order to obtain it.

A garden in the rear yard of your property is very simple to achieve and easy to maintain, too. Gardens with nutritious vegetables do much more than add a nice feature to your lawn.

They repay your labor efforts with healthy foods and a much more varied and wholesome diet.

Vegetable gardeners are in tune with their surroundings. They return to Earth what they take out of its soil.

A prosperous and lush back garden may impact your life greatly and positively, whilst also rewarding your expertise with a healthy supply of nutrients.

If you are interested in a new chemical and pesticide-free garden you should look to create one in the rear yard of your house.

It could be a terrific activity for the family and a very enjoyable experience for your children.

They might love to assist you as you get along with your accomplishment.

We can provide you with a number of easy strategies for beginners so that you promptly understand the best way to achieve the best gardening techniques, with no expertise or very little expertise, whether you are a novice, an amateur, or a vegetable-gardening beginner.

Planting your own vegetable garden enables you to keep control of any harmful substances used on foods, get fresh veggies to eat raw or cook during the harvesting period.

It also saves you pennies both in winter and summer allowing you to freeze or preserve your vegetables for use throughout the year.

INTRODUCTION

Vegetable gardening includes choosing a site, planning the garden, preparing the soil, selecting the plants and seeds, planting a crop, and cultivating the plants until they are ready for harvest. The final result is a new product to consume, share, or market.

Anyone who's willing to spend some time every day or every other day to nurture the crops may grow a vegetable garden. It does not take a good deal of cash, time, or ability, though some of each will be useful. With practice and patience, your abilities will improve each year. Do not be discouraged if the first effort is not a massive success.

Growing veggies needs a certain amount of space, but not always acres. A vegetable garden may be on the floor or within a planting bed, however, it does not need to be. Many vegetables can be raised in containers. For instance, sufficient lettuce for a salad could be raised with a 12-inch kettle on the rear deck. Insert several radishes and carrots, also raised in 12-inch containers and you get a fantastic start on a yummy salad.

Success, however, takes more than space for your vegetables to grow. They need sun, water, atmosphere, soil, fertilizer, and maintenance.

CHAPTER 1 - HOW TO START BUILDING A HAPPY AND HEALTHY RAISED-BED GARDEN

Site Selection

Select a convenient site in total sunlight with easy accessibility to water and abundant, well-drained soil. Avoid areas near trees and huge trees which will compete with all the garden for sun, water, and nutrition. You will want to put in your garden in an accessible place within close distance of water supply and storage space for watering cans and gardening resources. Sunlight is very important for your own garden to flourish since plants convert light energy to chemical energy. Pick a place that gets the maximum exposure to the morning sun. South-facing gardens are better since they get some sunlight throughout the day.

Success, however, takes more than only somewhere to grow the vegetables. They need sun, water, atmosphere, soil, fertilizer, and maintenance.

Sunlight

Most vegetables need eight hours of direct sun, like plants which we raise because of their leaves--such as spinach, lettuce and chard--plants and crops we raise due to their storage roots (for example, radishes, turnips, and beets) could be raised in no more than six hours of sun but do considerably better when exposed for eight hours or longer. Plants which we grow for their fruit, such as tomatoes, squash, and cucumbers, want at least eight hours of direct sunlight but they perform better with 10 hours.

Water

One of the most significant facets of gardening is water, which constitutes 90 percent of plant weight. Water is heavy and hard to maneuver, so track down the garden near a potable water source, which makes it effortless to water the lawn correctly. Dragging a hose countless feet or taking buckets of water throughout the lawn every couple of days makes using a garden much more work. Normally, vegetables require one inch of water weekly, and you want to provide just what isn't provided by rain. Water the soil, not the plant, because most diseases are spread by water splashing on the leaves. Overwatering can also cause pest and disease problems in addition to washing away nutrients and converting a precious garden source into pollution in neighboring streams.

Planning

Gardening is not as simple as simply planting a seed and transplanting plants. After having chosen a site, there'll be other questions to take into account in the preparation stage. The size of your garden is going to be restricted by the dimensions of your lawn. You will want to construct garden beds in narrow rows so that you have room to attend the plants without even stepping on or harming the plants nearby. It is possible to sketch out your design beforehand or put down things to picture the distance. If you do not have sufficient space for a huge vegetable garden, do not worry. A three-meter by three-meter garden is adequate, and you may also grow vegetables in containers in your own balcony if you don't own a garden.

WHAT KIND OF GARDEN?

You could go for raised beds, container gardens, conventional rows, or intensive plantings.

Container gardens: Lots of vegetables can be raised in containers that are heavy enough to contain their own root systems. Containers may vary from as little as a 12-inch flowerpot to some half whiskey barrels. The larger the container, the more likely it is to succeed, and the bigger the plant, the bigger the container should be. Vegetables that do well in containers are, among others: beans, beets, carrots, collards, cucumbers, eggplants, garlic, spinach, leeks, lettuces, leafy greens, peas, peppers, lettuce, lettuce, squash, Swiss chard, and berries. Mix and match veggies in 1 container for elongated crop and beauty. Containers require more frequent irrigation than blossoms, particularly since the plants develop and need more water. A trickle irrigation system attached to a timer is a fantastic addition to your container garden.

Raised beds: An assortment of materials can be utilized to build raised beds, but don't use materials that may leach chemicals to the ground, for example, older railroad ties. The soil in raised beds will heat rapidly in the spring and keep warm longer in the fall. Vegetables in raised beds may need more frequent irrigation compared to those within an in-ground garden. Once implanted and planned properly, 1 4-foot by 8-foot raised bed may provide a fantastic selection of products for a couple of people. The implementation of trellises supplies vertical gardening and raises the area accessible to vining plants such as cucumbers and beans.

Use intensive gardening methods to maximize the use of the space. Succession planting may also assist in optimizing the harvests out of a bed that is raised in a little location.

In-ground gardens: Larger places allow gardeners to select traditional row gardening. Even though a row garden is simpler to handle a tractor for planting, harvesting, and other garden chores, planting at a bed makes better use of space. Utilizing beds allows you to plant many rows closer together and to shade bud seeds preventing them from climbing later in the season. Beds may call for a little more labor to plant initially, but when implanted properly, beds can decrease the demand for weeding later in the season. You might even incorporate vegetables on your decorative beds.

Whichever garden type is selected, start small. Only plant in the total amount of space that is possible to manage. The garden ought to be fun and intriguing, not a job to be dreaded and avoided. Start small, enhance the soil, handle the weeds, and also enlarge the garden as your abilities and interests grow.

WHAT TO PLANT?

Grow what you prefer to consume. If space is restricted, focus on veggies that yield the best return for the attempt, such as beans, pole, tomatoes, root crops, and leafy greens. Should you prefer to cook odd foods, attempt vegetables that are hard to discover or expensive on the market--for example specialty lettuces or broccolini. Now that your garden is plotted outside and you've chosen some nutrient-rich soil, it is time to select what to plant. Start with what you want to eat -- what could you add to a new summer salad along with a hearty winter stew? Spring is a superb time to plant broccoli, tomatoes, spinach, carrots, beets, and cucumbers. In North Carolina most veggies have been raised as annuals, however, a few biennials and perennials are also raised. Vegetables are grouped by the way they develop:

- Cool-season annuals. Plant these plants in early spring and early autumn. They're cold-hardy and flourish in spring and autumn when temperatures are below 70°F: beets, broccoli, Brussels sprouts, cabbage, lettuce, cauliflower, collards, kale, kohlrabi, lettuce, mustard, onions, peas, celery, radishes, rutabagas, spinach, Swiss chard, and turnips.

- Warm-season annuals. Plant these plants after spring frost, once the lands have heated up. They're frost-sensitive and flourish in summer when temperatures are over   70°F: cantaloupes,   beans, cucumbers, okra,   peppers,   pumpkins, southern   peas,   squash,   corn,   sweet potatoes,   tomatoes,   eggplant,   and watermelons.

- Biennial   plants.   One   example   is artichokes: they grow during the initial season, and then they blossom, fruit, and perish the next year.

- Perennial   crops,   like   asparagus   and rhubarb,   endure   several   years   after established.

When   to   plant?   Strategy   for   yearlong production through succession planting.
   o Spring.   Plant   cool-season   plants early   and   warm-season   plants   in

late spring. Utilize a cold frost or frame cloth to start earlier in this season.

- o Summer. Cool-season plants will bolt since the days lengthen and temperatures rise. Use shade fabric to protect crops and expand the season. Warm-season plants planted in late spring could rise before the first fall frosts. In late summer, plant cool-season plants for fall.
- o Fall. Cool-season plants established in late summer may keep growing through medium to freezing temperatures.
- o Winter. Cold hardy crops (like kale, collards, and turnip greens) implanted in autumn may live through winter. In colder locations, use a cold frame or suspend fabric to prolong the season.

Scheduling when to plant and when to crop can be carried out in many powerful ways. Writing down planting days and harvest dates on a calendar is a technique employed by a number of farmers and anglers. Another possibility is drawing a diagram of the garden and composing projected planting and harvesting dates onto the garden diagram. Understanding when an area is going to be chosen helps with preparing when to plant a different crop in that area. Employing this technique of preparation allows for a small space to be handled to its fullest capacity.

HOW TO ORGANIZE THE GARDEN?

- Plant in rows, then run them around the incline of the property to decrease erosion. When there's little if not any slope, north to south orientation gets the best use of the sun. When planting, bunch tall plants (corn, okra, and sunflowers) and trellised vines (peas and beans) on the north side of the garden so that they will not shade shorter plants.

- Don't nurture the buildup of disease and insect germs by developing the very same forms of plants at precisely the exact same area every year. Rather, organize a harvest rotation for every garden or bed space to stop crops in precisely the exact same plant family from being implanted in precisely the exact same area in series.

Possessing a garden strategy makes it easier to decide what seeds or transplants to buy, just how many will be required, and if they'll be required. Maintaining a garden journal together with preceding garden strategies is a fantastic way to document what worked and what did not. One part of garden preparation consists in moving over what's been employed before and what has not, so further mistakes could be avoided later on. Matters to record from the garden diary could include a listing and map of that which had been planted, planting dates, types, source of crops, soil and air temperatures throughout the growing season, soil test results, pesticides and fertilizers applied, rain received, and dates and amount of harvest. It's also helpful to include photographs throughout the season

PREPARING THE SOIL

Containers: Buy potting soil or create your own by mixing equal parts of compost, shredded pine bark mulch, and vermiculite. Don't use garden soil in container gardens. Vegetable gardens flourish using nutrient-rich garden soil. Particularly if you're just beginning with gardening, Blue Cube is a handy no-mess approach to obtain the highest quality garden dirt delivered to your door. Blue Cube's Premium Garden Soil is a blend of black soil, mulch, sand, natural fertilizer, and lime. This diatomaceous land is just formulated to match your climate and conditions, placing your own vegetable garden in the very best position to be successful.

Raised beds or in-ground garden: Amend your soil with organic material first (either homemade mulch or bought licensed mulch). Then submit a soil sample to ascertain the pH and nutrient content of your soil. N.C. Cooperative Extension center in your county can offer a soil test kit to have your soil analyzed and acquire certain recommendations for growing veggies. Amend the soil as recommended in the soil investigation

Planting

Space plants based on the tag on the seed package or plant label. Permit space for the plant to grow, also leave room for airflow between crops to reduce illness.

Plant seeds just two to twice as deep as the best diameter of the seed. Enclose the seed and push the soil lightly to guarantee good seed-to-soil contact. For crops in peat cubes or cups, remove the region of the peat container that's over the potting soil in the container, and make sure you cover the containers nicely with soil when placing them from the garden. Acclimate transplants for their new surroundings by giving temporary color for tender transplants for a couple of days after putting out them.

Mulching enhances the conservation of soil moisture, reduce weeds, and decrease erosion. Use shredded leaves, pine straw, paper, or some other organic material that will break down and enhance the soil.

A strategy for continual harvest consists in staggering planting dates in a single - to two-week intervals. As an instance, if you're likely to plant four servings of lettuce, then plant the initial week, the next week, the week after that, and also the fourth week.

SEEDS OR TRANSPLANTS?

Each planting process has advantages.

Seeds: A much larger assortment of seeds is accessible compared to transplants, and seeds are less costly. Some seeds may be sown directly into the garden. Plant seeds according to package instructions. You can even develop your own transplant by planting seeds. Six to eight months prior to the transplanting date, sow the seeds according to packet instructions into a container inside or in a cold period, greenhouse, or other shielded growing structure. Gently transition seedlings in the secure environment to the garden, off them by gradually introducing the transplant into complete sunshine for a longer period every day over a week.

Transplants: You can begin a garden fast with transplants and harvest plants sooner compared to seeds. Small plants bought from a garden center, catalog, or internet supply a means to overcome seasonal restrictions. Some crops require so long to grow that if started from seed in the garden at the start of the year, they'd still not be ready to harvest at the close of the year (Brussels sprouts, as an instance).

Except for berries, which may be planted slightly deeper, transplants should be planted in the ground at exactly the exact same depth they were from the container. Some negative effects of using transplants include the greater cost in comparison to seeds, along with the restricted number of types. Also, root plants (like carrots, radishes, and beets) don't transplant well.

Garden Care

If it does not rain, water fresh seeds and transplants daily until they grow. Water older plants as necessary. Frequency depends on rain and temperature. Examine the ground for moisture, and also see crops for signs of drought stress (leaves drooping at the daytime or early evening). Soil from the vegetable garden ought to be kept moist but not muddy. Knowing the kind of dirt in your garden can allow you to figure out how often it needs to be watered. A soil that's heavy with a lot of clay will have to be watered less often compared to a soil which is lighter with a lot of air pockets, like a sandy soil or container garden dirt.

Fertilize just as needed subsequent to the recommendations on your own soil investigation. Compounds with long growing seasons, such as corn and berries, may need extra fertilizer partway throughout the growing season. Watch for signs of nitrogen and other nutrient deficiency (such as leaves turning yellow and slow expansion). Avoid the desire to overfertilize, which may create lush plant growth, but it may reduce flowering and fruit growth and grow pest issues.

Mulch to keep moisture and manage weeds. 1-2 inches of weed-free loose mulch (like grass clippings — seed-free —, shredded leaves, pine bark mulch and wheat straw) or five to six layers of paper should be sufficient to keep down weeds and to keep the soil moist.

Expand the growing season by protecting plants from extreme cold and hot weather. Use mulch to moderate soil temperatures. Cold eyeglasses shielded by a row protect produce color for heat-sensitive plants. Covered with frost fabric, cold frames protect plants through freezing temperatures.

CHAPTER 2 - PEST AND DISEASE MANAGEMENT

Pests are drawn to stressed crops, so try to keep plants content and healthy with sufficient sunlight, water, and fertility.

Input flowering plants that encourage beneficial insects to control pests and help pollination.

Select hardy disease and pest-resistant plants or seeds by studying labels carefully. By way of instance, tomato seed and plant labels which have VFN indicate a number resistant to verticillium wilt, fusarium wilt, and nematodes. When picking transplants, start looking for the ones that are free of pests and diseases.

Water the soil and root region, but never the leaves. Soaker hoses and trickle irrigation will decrease standing water to the foliage, and which contributes to foliar diseases. Avoid splashing dirt, and some other ailments it may take, on the leaves.

Scout the garden: Analyze plants often for damage or disorder, including the bottom of leaves, and intervene early. Make sure you also check at nighttime when slugs and snails are outside. Most caterpillars are the exact same color as the foliage, so look carefully for the insect and for frass (the residue left by a pest after it eats plant components). Learn how to differentiate plant-harmful-pests and beneficial insects such as pollinators like bees that assist fruit collection, predators like ladybird beetles which eat pests and parasitic insects like small wasps that lay eggs onto pests.

Remove dead and diseased plants and drop in the trash - eliminate the weeds before they flower. Do not let weeds go to seed!

Practice crop rotation - pests and ailments can develop in the dirt nearby host plants. Reduce insect and disease issues every year by rotating the places where yearly vegetables have been planted.
 Learn more about the plants being raised - know what's normal and what may develop into an issue. Particular crops are vulnerable to certain pests. By way of instance, skillet frequently gets vine borers. Broccoli, collards, and cabbages get cabbage loopers. And melons are vulnerable to fungus and other ailments. A gardener who understands the most probable diseases and pests for each harvest

will realize that it is simple to block or intervene quickly when problems arise.

Use the least toxic pest control plan available. When using pesticides, remember to be kind to bees by not spraying plants while they're blooming and just spraying in the late day. Watering is among the key components of keeping a vegetable garden. Water deeply from the morning. Pull weeds out regularly. Order organic mulch at a cube and employ involving the vegetable rows to shield from weeds. Maintain a watchful eye out for invasive pests and diseases.

Just like this, you've come to be a gardener. Enjoy delicious and fresh vegetables from your garden by following these simple steps. Keep together with challenges going to the vegetable garden daily or two times a day. Eliminate weeds, pest infestation, and diseased plants once the issue first arises, before the problem spreads.

WHEN TO HARVEST

Plants produce fruit and vegetable seeds to replicate. After a plant generates mature fruits, it stops putting energy into breeding. (The plant stops making blossoms and fruits) If the fruit is eliminated before it fully develops, then the plant will attempt again, making more fruits. Many plants produce so fast that they have to be harvested each day or two. These include okra, string beans, garden peas, cucumbers, summer squash, and tomatoes. Daily garden visits guarantee veggies will be chosen at the summit of perfection and not permitted to become overripe or spoiled, bringing insects or animal scavengers.

Start looking for indications that animals have been in the garden (for example, footprints and droppings, which may pose a health hazard by harboring parasites and disease organisms). Eliminate vegetables and fruits which might have come in contact with animals and their feces.

The simpler the garden is to view and access, the more likely it's going to be seen on a regular basis.

CHAPTER 3 - THE ADVANTAGES OF RAISED BED GARDENS AND HOW EASILY THEY CAN BE CREATED

A bed that is raised, by definition, is a garden bed that's built up rather than down, to some position that simplifies all types of gardening challenges. You are able to create raised beds by simply heaping soil into a heap, or simply by using boxes to enclose and include garden dirt. Garden boxes tend to be interchangeable with raised beds since a few retaining wall or substance almost always needs to be utilized as a way to keep the integrity of the bed as time goes on.

No Tilling is best for your Soil

A raised bed is actually a means of preparing your dirt for the simplest possible gardening—the 'no job ' type. Rather than tilling up the dirt from year to year in order to add fertilizer and adjustments, anglers usually keep their beds that are raised simply by incorporating substances at the top. Compost, mulches, manures and other soil conditioners can go right on the top couple inches of the ground with no necessity for work. And the dirt is capable of accomplishing its own tilling as roots and worms push through. While routine tilling by individual hands will deplete the soil construction, doing nothing builds the natural part of your soil.

Your Back Can Thank You

It is surprising just how much knee and back strain can occur by taking care of a garden, particularly a big one, and this may have a severe toll with time. A raised bed, especially those who are 12" tall, fix debilitated joints and back pain. Even young men and women who are thinking about farming as a livelihood choice should consider the possible harm to their back that organic farming may cause them by hand weeding. Contemplate raised beds as an investment in your health.

Raised Beds Appear Nicer

This may look like pure vanity, however having nicer beds may have a practical function. In town, particularly if you're attempting to start off with a vegetable garden, a raised bed might be a requirement for keeping neighbors content. Raised beds make pathways only a tiny bit simpler to keep clean and tidy since there's a definitive line between the bed and the trail.

Raised Beds Help Keep Out Critters

Slugs can climb. However, the tall sides of a garden box offer a chance to change their tracks and prevent them from going into your garden. Many anglers swear that slugs will not crawl over copper flashing, which may edge your box. You might even put in hardware fabric around the bottom of the box to stop crawling monsters such as groundhogs from slipping root plants. And, due to their height, dogs are less likely to urinate directly in your plants. If deer are a problem, you may add deer fencing straight to your bed, or buy a box using a built in deer fence. It's also much easier to add vinyl decoration to elevated garden beds such as bird obstacles, cold frames, or row covers.

Raising Your Own Soil Means Much Better Drainage

In areas likely to flood, or in marshy yards, a garden bed could be the only method to have a complete growing season. The popular thickness to get a raised bed is 11", that can be just one inch under the sides of a 12" high garden box. For many plants, this is sufficient drainage, and supplies plant nearly a foot of additional breathing space over moist conditions. Raised beds also tend to drain in general, even in heavy rains.

You may have fewer weeds and crabgrass

Tilling really creates weeds by burying bud seeds and providing them an ideal chance to disperse. Raised bed manufacturers swear by covering their beds with mulch, cardboard, black vinyl from the spring to destroy all of the plants that grew up from the winter. If it is time to start planting again, just rake off the dead weeds before they have an opportunity to go to seed. Among the very best tactics to combat crab bud is using a bed. Install a weed barrier at the base of beds at 10" high to prevent the grass from infiltrating.

You are able to plant raised beds sooner in the summer largely because of their greater drainage from the soil, the dirt dries out quicker in the spring and also warms more rapidly for planting, compared to dirt at floor level. Many anglers also find a surprising variety of crops have overwintered in a raised bed that shouldn't have been able to. Again, all of this has got to do with all the kind of dirt in the bed. In case untilled and fortified using compost, your soil will modulate temperatures better than upset, nutrient-poor soil. Bunk beds could be momentary

Renters who want to have a garden should begin the discussion with their landlord by showing them them a wonderful photograph of a bed. A neat, clean, and properly developed garden box may improve property values and also be a decoration rather than an eyesore. If the landlord says yes, a temporary garden could be constructed using a detachable garden box. The box is only set on the floor, the cardboard is placed above the bud indoors, and the box is full of soil. When you proceed, take the box, distribute the dirt, and toss bud seed again.

Raised beds prevent contaminated dirt

Urban gardeners are at a greater risk of eating heavy metals, such as lead. Many distinct vegetables, particularly roots, greens, and berries, consume heavy metals from contaminated soils and can result in a true threat. Placing beds away from the street, exploring previous uses of your property, and planting thick hedges can help, but raised beds offer the exceptional chance to bring new soil that has not been exposed to anything toxic that might be on the site. Toxicity can be greatly reduced with the addition of compost, diluting the levels of pollution from year to year, and transmitting heavy metals into soil particles (another amazing use for compost!).

Raised beds are excellent for beginners

Raised beds provide a simple way to begin gardening by eliminating many obstacles for novices. They require just a bit more investment in the beginning, however in lots of ways they guarantee achievements from the very first year. Insert a box, some dirt, some mulch, some seeds, some water, and something will expand. "Row crows" cannot boast the exact same achievement: the procedure isn't as apparent as the route that raised beds offer.

Raised Bed Garden Vs In-ground garden

A raised bed frame could be made from timber, masonry, or other construction materials. Raised beds may vary in size depending on the site, the substances utilized in their structure, and the personal taste of the angler. Raised beds are usually 6 to 8 inches high, 3 to 6 feet wide, and

6 feet to 8 ft. Some elevated bed frames are additionally raised over the floor with bricks or blocks to make them accessible to folks who have trouble bending or stooping.

For school and community gardens, there are lots of benefits of gardening in raised beds, such as:

- Manageability: Raised beds supply a manageable means to garden a more compact area.
- Prevention of soil compaction and plant harm: Some of the best benefits of raised beds stems from the security that the construction supplies from foot traffic, particularly from kids working in a garden area. Since individuals work on the trails and do not walk in well-designed raised beds, the dirt doesn't become compacted and crops are not as likely to be damaged.
- More growing season: Raised beds warm up more rapidly in the spring and also drain (assuming the land is properly prepared), allowing for an extended growing season and improved growing conditions. Especially in the South, a

correctly ready raised bed allows plant roots to grow.

- Less weeding and upkeep: when the dirt in a raised bed has stabilized, compaction is all but non-existent hence the demand for seasonal tilling is minimal. Weed populations decrease more than at a raised bed that's well cared for and mulched.
- Better drainage: A well-prepared raised bed enables the soil to drain better than at an in-ground garden. In some regions of Georgia, the soil drains poorly compared to raised beds, that instead allow gardening of plants that wouldn't grow.
- Easier dirt alterations: A raised bed can empower crop growth in a place that otherwise wouldn't support gardening. On steep slopes, raised beds can work as a kind of terracing. Raised beds may be constructed on a lot of compacted, difficult-to-garden urban lands. For certain plants that thrive particularly in lands, raised beds could be amended appropriately.
- Substance conservation: Since the gardening area is focused, the direction

of water, fertilizer, fertilizers, and soil amendments could be carefully controlled, resulting in less waste.

- Accessibility for gardeners with disabilities: Raised beds, in the appropriate elevation, can boost access for wheelchairs, or even for anglers that have difficulty bending over.
- Reduced Conflict: In gardens where plots are rented for the year, raised beds clearly specify boundaries and reduce inadvertent trampling.

In-Ground Garden

Gardening in the ground enables using tractors to initially prepare regions, as well as the startup prices, which are much lower compared to raised beds. Other benefits include:

- Utilization of present soil: Most lands are perfectly fine for gardening, given the soil is properly tilled, mulched, and watered. Even without organic amendments, many Georgia lands can make a bountiful harvest.
- Financially economical: Using existing dirt rather than minding soil, cash could be

stored and used for natural alterations that would be required to enhance even the soil that is compacted. As it's highly unlikely to locate real topsoil in Georgia, it's frequently superior to enhance what you have than import something fresh and potentially unknown. Purchased topsoil is generally either artificial (consisting mostly of sand and bark) or like the soil currently available on site. If amended correctly, clay soils have advantages that aren't found in man-made lands. If you're unsure of the level of your dirt or how to amend it, then take samples to the community county Extension agent for testing. When there's a possibility the soil was contaminated with potentially hazardous chemicals, then request to have the soil tested for heavy metals.

- Less startup work: A level, the well-drained area could be well prepared using a tractor or big roto-tiller.
- Less durable: An in-ground garden can easily be substituted with a different crop or transferred to a different place.
- Reduced water demands: In-ground beds will not dry out as fast as raised beds

and will consequently require less water to keep.

- Quicker irrigation: Concerning irrigation methods, in-ground gardens are easy to design and simple to install when compared with raised beds which require careful design and setup.

While there are lots of benefits to raised beds, in addition, there are some disadvantages. Bunk beds need the building of a wall or border restraint. Even though this is sometimes constructed with recycled materials, it requires extra work, at least initially. Raised beds that are raised are much more costly and require some amount of technology to support their weight. Raised beds also ought to be full of dirt, which may become costly and takes a fantastic comprehension of lands and soil amending.

Raised beds are somewhat more lasting than in-ground gardens, therefore planning for prospective usage is vital. Some plants aren't ideal for elevated bed production. By way of instance, sweet corn necessitates bigger blocks of crops to make sure proper pollination takes place. Watermelons have a tendency to overtake a little raised bed unless streamlined types are raised and possibly trellised. Ultimately, most raised bed gardens rely solely on hand labor for many tasks, such as planting, fertilizing, and weeding.

Before beginning a school or community garden, it's very important to think about which kind of garden is suitable for your present and future requirements and the number of resources and time your situation will need. Watch the other books in this series to learn more about planning, producing, and sustaining a community or school garden. While meal gardening is a superb activity to do in your lawn, it is also part of an increasing trend of people wanting to eat much better, develop some of their own meals, and have more control over the level of the food supply. What better way to make certain you eat healthy food than developing it yourself? In 2009, the National Gardening Association (NGA) finished a questionnaire that characterized food preservation in the USA. Here Is What it found:

✓ Around 23 percent, or 27 million Families, had a vegetable garden in 2008. That's two million over in 2007. The amount of meals drinkers rises to 31 percent or 36 million families, should you include those individuals growing veggies, berries, and herbs.

✓ The Average man spends roughly $70 in their food garden each year. The entire nationwide is $2.5billion spent on food gardening. I clarify what you gain out of this $70 compared to what you would spend in the supermarket later in this segment.

✓ The typical vegetable garden is 600 square Ft, but 83% of those vegetable gardens are less than 500 square feet. Almost half of the anglers grow some veggies in containers too.

✓ The average vegetable gardener is faculty educated, married, female, age 45 or older, and does not have any children at home. And nearly 60% of vegetable anglers have been gardening for under five decades.

✓ The typical causes of vegetable gardening in order of significance are: to generate fresh meals, to spend less, to generate better-quality meals, and also to grow food that you know is secure. (I go into detail about many critical reasons to develop food later in this chapter)

There you have it. A lot of food anglers are outside taking care of their plants, and the numbers are increasing quicker than wheat in July. You may grow just a little food garden, but when all of the gardens have been added together, the effect is huge. Want further evidence? Allow me to show you!

✓ About 36 million families grow veggies, fruits, berries, and veggies. The typical garden size is 600 square feet. The NGA quotes you could create about 1/2 pound of vegetables per square foot of lawn annually. That is about 300 lbs of veggies in the typical garden. The normal cost, in season, of veggies, is approximately $2 per pound, therefore the typical vegetable garden generates $600 value of produce. So, Americans spend an average of $70 to afford $600 value of product each year. Wow! That is a fantastic return in my novel!

✓ When you figure that the amounts nationwide, 36 million families spend $2.5 billion to yield a GNGP of over $21 billion worth of veggies every year. That is a stimulation plan I could live with! (Don't you think? Proceed to the section "Save cash" later in this chapter to determine how it is possible to save that type of money by growing your own veggies)

It improves your wellbeing

Most of us know we are supposed to consume more fruits and vegetables daily. It is not just great advice from your mother. Many vegetables are packed with vitamins A and C, fiber, water, and minerals like potassium. An increasing body of research demonstrates that eating fresh fruits and veggies not only provides your body with vitamins and nutrients needed to operate correctly but in addition, it shows that lots of fruits and veggies are packed with phytochemicals and antioxidants -- certain substances that help fight and prevent disease. While certain fruits and vegetables are high in certain nutrients, the best method to ensure to receive a fantastic variety of these chemicals on your diet would be to "consume a rainbow": by eating an assortment of different-colored veggies and fruits, you receive all the nutrients that you will need to be healthy.

It can help you save some money

You will have some savings by growing your own fruits and vegetables. In reality, based on the kind and amount you develop, it is possible to save tens of thousands of dollars. By spending several bucks on plants, seeds, and provides in spring, you are going to create veggies that produce pounds of produce summer. Rather than needing to go to the supermarket to purchase all that, you have produced it already for free in your own lawn. It is your personal produce section! You will save hundreds of dollars on your grocery bill every year by developing a garden. Here is just 1 instance of how a vegetable garden can help save you some money. In addition, I incorporate some strategies for series cropping and interplanting. While I suggest string crops, I am imagining two plants in a growing season. I am also assuming 8-foot-long raised beds with rows with distance to walk between the beds in the middle.

Help the Environment

Your tomatoes, lettuces, and melons in the supermarket store are priced more than just the cost necessary to produce them. It is projected that the typical product travels around 1,500 kilometers to get from farm to supermarket, and that is only fruits and vegetables produced in the USA. Increasingly, products have been imported from overseas countries, for example China and Chile. The fossil fuels used to transfer these vegetables has an impact on air pollution and global warming. So, among those big-picture causes of developing your own products is to combat these effects on earth. Additionally, by increasing your vegetables, fruits, and veggies, you also lower the total amount of pollution that is made on the farm. Despite it being a traditional or organic farm, lots of big farms tend to use a lot of fertilizers, pesticides, and herbicides to cultivate their crops. Regrettably, a number of those additives wind up as resources (and their production requires fossil fuels). By developing your own products working with a minimum amount of those inputs, you can cut back on the total amount of fertilizer and chemical contamination which ends up in waterways across the nation.

Raise your quality in life

A less tangible (but nevertheless significant) reason to cultivate your own vegetables is linked to wellbeing. Vegetable gardening is a superb way to unwind after a tough day. You are able to attain a very simple pleasure and pride in drifting throughout your garden, snacking to a bean and a cherry tomato there, pulling out a few weeds, watering, and enjoying the fruits of your labors. It is a quick, easy gratification in a world that often is complex and complicated. Furthermore, if you garden with other people in a neighborhood garden, you are going to create new friendships and bonds with your neighbors. According to the NGA food gardening poll, I explained earlier in this chapter, over a million neighborhood gardens exist across the nation. Frequently community gardens become a focus for local beautification, education, and improvement projects. If the gardens are sown, folks begin taking interest and pride in their area and the way it looks. Often graffiti, crime, and vandalism are reduced only by producing a garden where people can gather together. And you thought all you're doing is developing a few vegetables.

There are many real benefits of gardening in raised beds. Part of the allure is to make an ordered appearance to the garden. Section of those benefits is producing perfect conditions for crops so that they may be intensively managed to produce top yields in rather tiny places. The most attractive part for me is that it makes gardening easier. Raised beds also give the capability to cultivate flowers or food in regions that could otherwise be unsuitable.

Improves Requirements For Plants
- Grows Soil Depth
- Improves Soil Aeration
- Improves Soil Quality
- Prevents Soil from Compacting
- Longer Growing Season
- Greater Yields
- Bed Frames Support Trellises, Cold Frames, Covers, and Irrigation

Less Work and Easier accessibility for the Gardener
- Reduced difficulty
- Can work in the garden without getting dirty
- Access for the Physically Impaired
- Bunnies Can not Jump

Ability to Garden Unsuitable Sites
- Can Grow on Sites without Soil
- Can Grow on Sites Which Are too Steep
- Can Grow where Concerned about Soil Contamination

Requires Water
- Water Just the Beds, Not the Pathways
- Deep, Compost Soil Holds Moisture

Improves Conditions for Plants

There are several different environmental variables that determine how crops grow, but we may have the most positive impacts on plants by enhancing the dirt and controlling moisture. The building of a bed that is raised automatically allows for stronger lands and for improved drainage of wet soils. Soil aeration is enhanced as moist soils are emptied. In Spring, the dirt in a raised bed will heat faster than dirt at or below floor level, hence the climbing season is marginally more.

But just because dirt is thicker and better emptied, it does not automatically enhance soil quality. For this, we must take another step. My Grandfather used to say "do not plant a $5 plant at a 50 cent gap". What he meant was why pay $5 for a plant just to simply stick it on the floor with little or no preparation for your plant's achievement. The same goes for raised bed gardening. Just because we construct a raised bed does not automatically indicate that we'll have more veggies that we all know what to do with. To truly enhance the dirt, we actually must use the Dual Dig Method. This consists in melting the thickness of 2 shovels, approximately two feet, and combine peat moss and/or mulch to the native soil. This will make mild and well-aerated soils with a lot of pure nutrients.

Increases Soil Depth - deep fertile soil that's not compacted is partly achieved by constructing a wall or frame to grow the dirt above floor level. This can be further accomplished by digging to enhance the ground at least 2 feet deep.

Drains Soil - Provided that the raised beds aren't watered right, extra water will drain off, down to the floor level. I am certain that you have heard the term "Plant when soil is workable", but what exactly does it mean? This is all about the status of the dirt rather than about a date on the calendar. The dirt is starting to heat and isn't overly wet. It's not hard to turn over using a trowel or shovel and doesn't form clumps.

To check the dirt, grab a handful of soil, and squeeze it. If it crumbles, it is ready to operate. If it sticks together in a chunk, it's too moist or you also have too much clay. Sandy soil and dirt with a great deal of compost will remain prepared to operate before clay lands.

Allowing the soil to drain permits the dirt to be worked before. Adding compost, peat moss, as well as sand to clay soils, also enables the soil to be worked sooner.

Notice: Draining Soil is a sword that is pleated. If a raised bed helps dry the dirt in the spring, so it's also going to dry the dirt during the summer if you don't want it to be this dry. In ponds, which gets lots of rain, this won't be a large issue.

Where I live, we get just about 13-15 inches of rain per year, therefore it's an issue. I need to irrigate everything if I wish to develop anything apart from sagebrush. I like the notion of creating raised beds two feet deep, so dirt can be kept profound and aerated without needing to dig far down to the floor, but it would require an excessive amount of water to maintain the beds watered during July and August. So my raised beds are at most 12 inches over the floor which appears to be a great balance for the climate.

Enhances Soil Quality - The soil is enhanced since the elevated bed creates vertical distance to add compost and other organic matter into the garden dirt. Decomposition can happen quickly in soils which are equally moist and aerated.

Prevents Soil from Compacting - part of land quality is preserving the mild, profound aerated soils. So walking on the bed is a no. Maintaining beds to 4 feet or less may allow reaching someplace from the bed without stepping onto it. I have some beds which are broader than 4 feet. I have a walkway down the middle (8x10 bed) or that I put stepping stones or boards so that we never need to measure directly onto the ground. Walking around compacted soil isn't a huge deal since the dirt is already compacted. If you walk on freshly dug soil that's two feet deep with a great deal of organic matter, your footprint can elongate four or five inches. If you step on a plant that has been growing in that soil, a 5 or 4-inch indention may split all of the roots off one facet of the plant.

Quicker Growing Season - Beds allow dirt to be worked earlier in the summer because the dirt begins warming earlier from the bed compared to the soil at floor level. Greater Yields due to greater, deeper soil supply plants with loose, deep, well-drained, well-aerated soil - Greater yields per square foot can also be because we could intensively handle little raised beds.

A farmer who plants a crop in a 500-acre area plows it to interrupt to make mild aerated soil, however, he plows it using a 10-ton tractor that also compacts the soil. After the harvest is growing, he could simply check a small sample of this harvest to test for moisture, good growth, insects, or ripeness.

In little raised beds, heavy aerated soils are simpler to maintain. Just about any plant could be assessed at least a weekly basis for moisture, good development, insects, or ripeness. Any issues can be quickly viewed and adjusted. The whole bed can readily be watered or only a couple of plants that require water. A lone pest can be crushed or just one leaf with aphids may be dipped in soapy water before the infestation gets an opportunity to spread. Should you decide that a pesticide has to be properly used, you determine just how much is employed and which crops need it.

Bed Frames Service Trellises, Cold frames, Covers, and Irrigation -- A wooden bed frame produces a ready base to attach trellises, covers, or supports within the bed. In addition, I prefer to attach a drip line in straight rows on the interior of the bed frames with principles.

- Trellis
- Tomato Supports
- Service Bird netting
- Service For Substance or Plastic Sheeting
- Irrigation Drip Line
- Less Function and Easier Access for the Gardener

Reduces Maintenance - The physical edge of the raised bed prevents grass and weed roots from slipping into the bed. The heavy, loose soil makes yanking weeds easy and doesn't typically require grinding tools. When the beds are sparse, planting, weeding, and harvesting could be achieved within reach of this path. Pulling weeds out of mild, aerated soil isn't similar to pulling weeds out of compacted soil. In tough soil, the odds are that you might need to dig up the bud or you risk breaking off the plant, leaving the root behind to grow. In mild soil, the whole weed can just be pulled from the floor. As it isn't a chore, you'll discover that you're pulling a couple of tiny weeds once you locate them rather than making plans to pull weeds or hoe the pops for many hours the next day. In reality, I do not even have a hoe.

You can work in the garden without getting dirty -With most traditional row gardens, even when you head outside to plant, weed or crop, you change clothing, particularly your shoes, since you know that you will get dirty. Now do not get me wrong, you can get filthy when turning over the ground in a raised bed. However, for the most part, it is possible to stand out the elevated bed to do most gardening jobs without stepping onto the ground. Bear in mind, a part of the intention behind the raised bed is to save you from stepping onto the ground. If you have to step in the bed, put a board or stepping stone, in order to measure in precisely the exact same area each moment. This will keep the soil from compacting longer.

Access for Physically Impaired — raised beds may decrease stooping and bending and may be constructed to coincide with the comfortable height for someone in a wheelchair or somebody that uses a walker.

Bunnies Cannot Jump - I needed to bring this one up. I read an internet conversation about raised bed gardening. 1 man, new to gardening, did not have a lot of success the past season because of rabbits eating plants. Someone suggested to construct a bed that was raised high enough to place it out of range of those rabbits. They constructed a bed that seemed to be approximately two feet above floor level and maintained the elevated bed. This solved all of the issues brought on by rabbits, since "bunnies cannot really jump". Rabbits may jump. I've seen them do it, therefore I predict that this is not actually true, but maybe rabbits do not like to leap into a raised bed where they cannot observe the landing place. It appears to me that fencing or tiny cages are a less costly solution to having rabbits in a little garden bed, however, I do not have rabbits where I live today, so that I cannot test either way. I want to hear from anybody else who has eliminated rabbit problems with raised beds rather than fencing.

Ability to Garden Unsuitable Sites

Could grow on sites without Soil - In Cities, raised beds may be utilized on asphalt, concrete, extremely compacted locations as well as rooftops. Raised beds may also be set on exceptionally rocky or mountainous regions that otherwise would not be possible to plant a garden.

Can Grow on Sites Which Are overly Steep - Steep slopes aren't acceptable for conventional row gardening, but raised beds constructed such as terraces can create appropriate areas to plant life.

Concerns about Soil Contamination - As raised beds may be used on concrete locations or rooftops in towns, anyone that's worried about land contamination may still use the region to grow veggies. Raised beds may be utilized to maintain clean dirt along with a pond liner that may be utilized to make sure that the plant roots do not penetrate down to the polluted soil or stop the contamination from blending with the sterile soil.

Raised Bed Building Materials

After we opt to construct a raised bed, the next step is to decide what material to use.

Factors for Raised Bed Building Materials
- Functional and/or Visually Appealing
- Price of Materials

- Life Span of Material
- Hold dirt or provide a location to walk or sit
- Organic Prerequisites
- Does the material leach compounds or alter the pH?

Functional and/or Visually Appealing - I think my easy wooden and piled stone raised beds appear fine, but the beds are mostly built to be cheap and functional. The planting regions are restricted from the frames or stone as well as the pathways that have been linked with landscape cloth and crushed stone to help keep undesirable weeds and grass out and also to supply broad paths that are clean, comparatively dry and level.

We've all seen amazing stone landscaping and raised beds designed not just to look really pleasant, but also to be practical and that is going to endure for several decades.

Price of Materials - Few people grow tomatoes in their home to save cash. We can't compete with all the ag-industry for cost. We do it since the ag-industry can't supply the exact same fresh home-raised flavor and quality. I joke with family and friends about spending hundreds of dollars a pound simply to have home-raised tomatoes, but that's a massive exaggeration. Truth is, it makes more sense to me to invest just a little money, effort, and time on something that I will eat rather than mowing grass. If time, money and space were no object, the majority of us could have expert stone masons build beautiful rock "seat-walled" raised beds. But most people are unlikely to spend tens of thousands of bucks to get a rock raised bed as soon as an untreated timber raised bed may be constructed for less than $50.

Life Span of Material - Untreated wood will likely last a decade in my cold chilly climate, but might not survive more than a couple of years in warm and moist climates such as found at the Southern U.S. Pressure Treated Wood is likely to endure for 20 decades. Used railroad ties have been lost but will endure for a lot more years. Concrete blocks should persist for quite a while, but a few are delicate and will easily break if they aren't full of dirt or mortared in place. I also have seen some garden or landscape cubes that have escalated from freezing in approximately ten decades.

Hold dirt or provide a location to sit or walk A New trend in landscaping would be your Seat Wall. Why don't you construct a raised bed that appears and stays like a chair wall? A normal 2x12 board does a fantastic job of holding dirt inside the bed, but on the border, a single plank produces a bad seat. Additional timber may be connected to the tops of this elevated bed to make a better chair. Most authentic seat partitions are made from concrete, stone, or garden cubes.

Organic Prerequisites - A lot of people who begin raised bed gardening do this with the notion of growing a number of their own food which has little or no additives. If the garden is sprayed, they understand exactly what type, how much spray has been used, and if it was used. They might or might not buy into the entire "Organic" idea. I am not likely to get into all of the details, but I am aware that it's likely to possess Arsenic treated wood in contact with dirt, animals, or food and be Certified Organic from the Federal Government. I like the notion of knowing where my food comes from and that it hasn't yet been contested and doesn't have additives I do not want. But because the Federal Government is in control of the Organic

Program, it functions like everything else that the Federal Government touches. I'm not convinced we're getting what we pay for or have been led to think.

- The pressure treated timber available at most building supply stores will leach copper to the ground. Copper isn't a major deal in the dirt rather than a large problem to individuals, but it's a large problem in aquatic systems.
- Wood treated with Arsenic remains readily available for agricultural purposes leaches arsenic to the soil.
- Soil connected with concrete may have raised pH due to the lime in the cement. This is fantastic for a few plants but isn't great for plants that favor low pH.
- Metal substances can leach metals to the soil particularly at pH 5.5 or reduced - luckily, many plants prefer pH above 5.5.

Raised Bed Building Materials

I've seen various substances used to make raised beds. This list comprises those substances.

- Lumber - treated or untreated - some untreated wood such as cedar and redwood are naturally rust resistant

- Landscape timbers
- Railroad ties (creosote)
- Rock Or Stone; mortared or loose piled
- Concrete Cubes; mortared or piled
- Bricks; Mortared or piled
- Formed concrete
- Corrugated Metal and culverts
- Corrugated fiberglass
- Old Tires
- Additional Repurposed Materials

The beds are levelled if the property has a reasonable amount of incline. The untreated lumber of these raised beds has started to demonstrate just a small weathering, but they're still square and incredibly hardy. The timber was subjected to the weather for four complete years when these images were shot. They've changed little from the 2 years since then, so I anticipate they will continue at least 10 years in my climate. Notice our A-frame PVC Greenhouse was constructed in a few of the raised beds. I've observed livestock water troughs utilized as big containers or raised beds previously. They're somewhat expensive, but it seems as though they do the job well. A lot of folks advocate that holes have been drilled at the floor so water may escape, but I believe that could be an error in arid climates. Once holes have been drilled, they can't be readily undone. All these troughs have drainage holes. I'm sure with a little thought we can think of a much better way to drain surplus water and have a reservoir of water at the ground as with the majority of indoor planters.

Note: when the soil pH is lower than 5.5, then there might be a few leaching of metals to the ground. Luckily, most plants require soil pH above 5.5. The incline of your garden site is quite important and determines that the size, effort, or cost necessary to construct raised beds. In case the site is flat or if it slopes really little, you are able to build raised beds nearly any width and length so long as you've got space. If the slope is quite steep, you'll be restricted to constructing little frames if you don't move a great deal of dirt or construct stair-stepped beds. To quantify incline on a brief space, you may use a carpenters level and a right 8 or 10-foot plank. An easy string and line will measure incline over larger distances without needing to purchase or borrow a questionnaire level.

STEPS TO BUILD A RAISED BED

1. Measure and Cut Lumber

2. Pick Frame Orientation

3. Mark and Drill Pilot Holes

4. Attach with Screws

5. Attach Corner or angles Brackets for Added

Power (Optional)

Step 1: Measure and Cut Lumber
Depending on the size of your raised bed along with the dimensions of the timber you purchase, you might not have to generate any cuts, but generally, timber will have to get cut. Some construction supply shops will make these reductions for you. I have three 5x10 foot raised beds constructed from 2x12 timber. I purchased the timber in 10-foot lengths; therefore 3 boards were required for every framework. Just one 10-foot plank has been cut in half to every bed.

Step 2: Pick Frame Orientation.

Decide if you need the bed to be marginally more, drive screws through the 5-foot finish planks to the endings of the 10-foot boards, marginally broader, drive screws through the 10-foot boards to the ends of The 5-foot finish planks, or split the difference, begin at one corner, and then lap every plank towards the conclusion of the following board.

Measure 3: Mark and Drill Pilot Holes

Most timber framing is done only with nails and hammer, but screws using pre-drilled pilot holes are also used, this way the framework will fit tighter, live longer, twist less, and can help prevent the boards from dividing. Begin by indicating the diameter of the board on each end which is to be drilled, which means it's possible to drill holes near the middle of the plank. Use a drill bit that's slightly narrower than the screws you intend on using. A 1/8th inch drill bit is suggested for #10 screws at softwood. Drill the pilot hole through the surface of a single plank and throughout the conclusion of another board.

Step 4: Merge Frame with Screws

Be sure to use screws that are long enough to maintain the boards together for several decades. A two-inch screw may hold a 2x4 board for a very limited time, however, the twist thread, is #10 twist that's 3.5 inches long and should hold for several decades. After drilling the pilot holes, begin the screws and allow them to stretch about a quarter inch from every hole on the opposite side of the plank. That means you'll have the ability to feel if the screws inserted into the pockets on another board. Hold the 2 boards close together until every screw is tightened.

Step 5: (Optional) - Attach corner mounts for extra strength

There are various kinds of angle and corner mounts ,ranging from approximately 50cents to $15 which can add strength to the corners. Some are so powerful that they'd maintain the bed frame together without added screws, but the better ones are costly and need bolts to maintain the angles into the framework. If you assemble the framework correctly, with great exterior screws, then the framework will last for many decades with no further support.

Measures to Level and Square the Raised Bed Frame

1. Place Raised Bed Frame Close into the Closing Site

2. Square the Bed Frame

3. Utilize Level to Determine High and Low Locations

4. Dig High Spots Away and Fill Low Locations

5. Closing Check Frame for Square and Level

6. Back-fill around Bed Frame with Soil or Gravel.

Steps to Construct Stepped Raised Beds onto a Slope

1. Determine the Complete Quantity of Rising or dip on the Slope

2. Determine Size of Lumber Number of Measures to Negotiate the Slope

3. Construct Open-Ended Bed Frame Sections

4. Set Bed Frames in Position One at a Time

5. The amount and Square Bed Frames

6. Fasten Bed Frames Collectively

7. Back-fill around outside of Bed Frame with Soil or Gravel

8. Double Dig Soil

9. Insert Soil Amendments

10. Connect Drip Irrigation

Step 1: Determine the Entire Quantity of Rising or Fall on the Slope - It was a very simple job to assess the slope since the site of this newly raised beds was adjacent to the home and the total amount of fall was readily quantified by clarifying the siding. I've got a 6-foot flat and took measurements every 2 feet to determine how consistent the incline was. I measured the fall beside the home and also 3 ft away in the home. In cases like this, the entire fall was approximately 32 inches in the top end of the bed that is projected to the lower end.

Step 2: Determine Size of Lumber and Number Of Measures to Negotiate the Slope - When I had 32-inch-wide planks, I could assemble one

14-foot framework to degree the area. But that would signify the top end of that framework would need to be dug nearly 32 inches down to the floor and the side could have 32inches of framework subjected to the sun, which might need to be watered constantly in the Summer. A slope is the best place to construct stair-stepped raised beds.

Step 3: Construct Open-Ended Bed Frame Sections - I decided to construct the stepped raised beds with timber rather than concrete blocks. I intended to make 3 stepped beds approximately 3 feet wide and 14 feet long with 2x12 lumber. I left a four-inch distance between the home and the raised bed to maintain the negative of the home dry. I also did not need to have the bed to expand beyond the cellar window wells, so that the 36-inch first strategy shrunk by four inches to 32 inches. I constructed the frames together with the outer diameter that is 32 inches, which makes the interior bed frame cuts 29 inches. I constructed 2 frame segments four feet long and a single segment in 62 inches. I chose this span simply to make the best use of my present 10-foot timber (62+29+29 = 120). So the final length of this stepped bed was 13 feet two. The top measure can be finished using a smaller board or it may be inserted after leveling.

Step 4: Place Bed Frames in Position One at a Time - Set the first elevated bed frame section to position near the peak of the incline to indicate where the soil has to be eliminated to level the framework segment.

Step 5: Amount and Square Frames - Put the framework section aside and start eliminating dirt. As there's a certain perennial side, it's not difficult to determine low and high places. The dirt on the side is divided and the dirt is slowly pulled out leaving trenches to your raised bed section to match into frames. If the uphill end of the bed frame segment is left open, be careful to maintain the box square. I attached a furring strip to maintain the box and replaced it and shut the close of the box using a part of 2x4. After either side of the frame, the segment is flat and the framework can also be flat from side to side, then add another frame segment and continue.

Step 6: Fasten Frames Collectively - After the bed frames are backfilled with dirt on the exterior of this framework and full of compost on the interior of the framework, the frames must be quite hardy, but until that time, the bed frames a mere sitting level in the ground. To add durability to each of the bed frame segments, use angles, and attach the frame segments.

Soil Planning - Dual Dig Method - Dig two shovel-lengths down. This necessitates the upper layer of dirt to be put into the side so that you may reach another layer down. If you would like to keep the place clean, put the dirt on a tarp, landscape cloth, or massive pieces of cardboard. Then dig the next amount of dirt, which may remain in place or be removed to make it much easier to combine. The soil always has to be turned, divided, and blended well with compost or sphagnum moss. Additionally, I added high dirt in my beds since it comprises sand, which can be also compost and helps break up the clay dirt. Start incorporating the initial dirt back in the bed and combine more mulch as you move. Depending upon how severe you get, this can combine, aerated, and insert new mulch to soil in 1-2 feet deep. The more time and effort you spend on this, the better.

Since my inherent soil has numerous clods and stones, I constructed a framework and attached 1/2 inch welded wire with furring strips and screws. The display eliminates all stones, clods, and sticks bigger than 1/2 inch. A little thumping the bigger clods divides them into smaller bits and enables them to pass through the monitor. It's possible to add mulch before the soil blend is very near the peak of the raised beds. As time passes, the soil level will settle. Considering that the soil line in my bed was approximately four inches from the top until I began digging, I estimate that the bed may hold about 16.5 cubic feet (CF) of fresh compost and other soil amendments. In the practice of digging, I eliminated another two or three CF of big stones. During the mixing process, I added around 20 CF of compost, sphagnum moss, and topsoil to the bed, but once I finished adding, mixing, and placing all of the eliminated topsoils back into the bed, the dirt is rounded off over the amount of the bed. I estimate that the mixing procedure added about 15 CF of atmosphere to the ground. So plan accordingly, simply replacing and removing the same dirt will include about 4 inches into a 50 square footbed.

How Safe Is A Pressure Treated Wood On Your Garden?

There have been many worries and a lot has been written about chemicals used in the treatment of wood in contact with vegetables. Before 2003, timber was treated with chromate copper arsenate (CCA), which can be poisonous as well as the EPA issued warnings regarding touching arsenate treated timber. There's been a wrong belief that the EPA prohibited the sale of timber treated with chromate copper arsenate (CCA) in 2003 (12/31/2003). Not correct. CCA treated timber is no longer qualified for a residential structure, but it's still qualified for sale for industrial, agricultural, and commercial applications. The odds are any treated timber you purchase now at your regional building supply store is among those newest EPA approved alternatives to CCA:

- Alkaline Copper Quaternary (ACQ)
- Copper Azole (CA)
- Micronized Copper Quaternary (MCQ)

However, you need to make sure before purchasing it. I read in a few gardening forums that the new treated timber products are safe to use for garden bed frames, however, I had to find information myself.

Alkaline Copper Quaternary (ACQ) - The Copper is the major active ingredient and can be described as being comparable to compounds used to maintain swimming pools clean and chiefly prevents bacterial growth. The Quat formula is comparable to some other bio-degradable cleaners and additives and has been a back up for copper resistant parasites.

There are no EPA recorded carcinogens in ACQ. Research has not identified any direct risks to people, but the goods do leach copper, which is extremely poisonous in aquatic systems. Brand Names include Yella wood, Preserve, and Nature Wood.

Copper Azole (CA) - Using ACQ, copper is the main component (98 percent) and also the tebuconazole fungicide is that the backup (<1 percent). Brand titles are Wolmanized, Tanalith, or Tanalised and Residential Outdoor.

Micronized Copper Quaternary (MCQ) - This is the same chemical formula as ACQ, however, it's first ground into tiny cubes (micron-sized) that are later injected into the cellular structure of the wood under high pressure. This procedure releases 90-99percent less aluminum into the surroundings, which is fantastic news for aquatic surroundings.

MicroPro asserts that the small quantity of copper that's discharged, binds immediately to natural chemicals in the soil, which makes it biologically inactive. The MCQ treated timber doesn't reveal as much color change as other treatment procedures. It's also somewhat less corrosive to fasteners as ACQ or CA treated timber, but you'd still utilize attachments that are approved. Since less corrosive doesn't imply non-corrosive. Brand names for MCQ treated timber comprise Yellawood MCQ, MicroPro, and SmartSense.

Copper Corrodes Hardware

Considering that wood preservatives utilize copper, treated timber is more inclined to respond and rust regular nails, screws, and other fasteners. Building codes have started to need stainless steel, ceramic coated, or hot-dipped galvanized fasteners to prevent failures due to corrosion when using the ACQ, CA, or MCQ treated timber products.

Treated Wood

Another consideration with wood is that the treatment procedure also pushes water back into the wood as it implements the compound therapy. Considering that the timber might nevertheless possess a higher moisture content it might shrink, warp and split as it dries.

Security Precautions

We're constantly cautioned to wear gloves, dust masks, and eye protection when cutting and handling both treated and untreated wood. We're additionally advised to wash our hands after handling the newest kinds of treated timber, wash garments individually, and are warned to not burn treated timber or use it.

Utilizing Untreated Wood

Am I convinced it is safe to make use of the aluminum treated wood products for elevated garden beds? Yes, it's safe for individuals, but it isn't safe for aquatic functions. The new micronized procedure is much better and leaches 90 percent less copper back to the surroundings compared to CA or ACQ methods. In the time of this writing, my untreated timber frames have been in the soil for between 4 - 6 decades. Yes, they've weathered and there are a couple of indications of rust to the timber that's underground, but they're still very solid and sound and I hope to have another 4 or 5 years until I must pull up and replace them.

The cold, dry climate which makes it difficult for me to grow veggies also slows down the decomposition rate of untreated wood. Untreated wood might not survive so long on your climate.

For me, 10+ years of usage of the expensive, untreated timber is a fantastic outcome. Also, I enjoy the expression of the untreated wood better, although the new micronized procedure appears more natural. When I had to pick, I'd utilize the Micronized Copper Quaternary (MCQ) treated timber. While leaching copper to the soil might not be all bad, leaching 90% less could be better.

ORGANIC FARMING

I read lately that organic farmers couldn't announce they create "Organic" when they'd treated timber that contacted their lands or animals. According to research, figurines (visit § 205.206 & § 205.602 below*) that govern the use of wood beneath the Organic Food Production Act. The true terminology in § 205.206 refers simply to arsenate substances in replacement and new installations, to not present installations. After further study, it seems that existing installations that use even arsenic established pressure treated timber are "grandfathered". So it's still possible for accredited Organic Vegetables to be made in raised beds constructed in arsenate treated wood when they obtained their certificate before December 31, 2003.

Additionally, since CCA treated timber remains approved for sale for agricultural applications, the chance exists that the plants or animals we consume could come in touch with fresh resources of arsenic. You don't think so? Who is responsible to make sure that it doesn't happen? This is another reason why we must all know the people who create and deliver our meals. Who does it make more sense? The local farmer who understands their livelihood is dependent upon their capacity to meet us as customers? Or the USDA, FDA, and EPA, that are seemingly responsible to nobody and not liable for anything?

CHAPTER 4 - DETAILED TO-DO LISTS IN VEGETABLE GARDENING

Dear Reader

I am an emerging writer and, with the sales made from the book, I can continue my studies to publish other books on the subject. I would appreciate an honest review from you.

Join Kimberley Smith newsletter to be informed about new books: kimb.smith.books@gmail.com

Thanks for your support

OTHER PUBLICATIONS BY KIMBERLEY SMITH

Raising Chickens For Eggs:

The Beginner's Guide To Building A Chicken-Coop, To Learn How to Raise A Happy Backyard Flock.   A Homesteading Solution While You Are At Home

HOW TO UTILIZE CROP ROTATION IN RAISED BED GARDEN

Vegetables, over most other kinds of plants, are vulnerable to diseases and pests; left unattended, these nuisances multiply exponentially. Crop rotation is an effective way of combating a plethora of plant maladies.

BASICS OF CROP ROTATION

The idea of crop rotation trusts in the gardener's understanding of vegetable plant households and their associated insects and quirks. Rotation means not developing the same or a related harvest in precisely the same area in consecutive years, which will help decrease the buildup of illness germs and insects. Experts recommend a five-to seven-year rotation cycle, and this, in theory, means that a garden must include five to seven raised beds. The gardener plants every raised bed using another crop annually before the cycle comes full circle.

Raised Bed Rotation Challenges

Notably in small arenas, using a sizable number of beds that are raised is impractical and crop rotation has to be approached creatively. For many folks, tomatoes (Lycopersicon esculentum) will be the singular motive to nurture a vegetable garden, but they along with other members of the nightshade family such as peppers (Capsicum annuum), potatoes (Solanum tuberosum) and eggplant (Solanum melongena) can't be raised in precisely the same region from year to year without illness finally turning into a severe issue. Soil replacement is a costly but workable alternative, as is choosing disease-resistant varieties. In a smaller garden, abstaining from developing a specific crop another year is just another approach to keeping healthy crop rotation.

Sample Planting Plan

With some careful planning and great record keeping, a garden can have great harvest rotation with as many as four raised beds. In every succeeding year, plant crops from 1 bed in the subsequent one from the line. By way of instance, at a four-bed garden, the very first frame might include onions (Allium cepa) and spinach (Spinacia oleracea) from the spring, berries in the summer and beans (Phaseolus vulgaris) from the autumn. Another frame may hold spring cabbage (Brassica spp.), summer squash (Cucurbita spp.) and decorative corn (Zea mays) from the autumn. In the next stage, a spring cover harvest such as yearly rye (Secale cereale) will be accompanied by peppers in the summertime and garlic (Allium sativum) in the autumn. The fourth bed could be implanted with peas (Pisum sativum), followed by sweet corn in summertime and turnips (Brassica Rapa) in autumn.

Supplementing Raised Beds

In areas where lots of multiple beds are somewhat impractical, using big containers to mature individual plants is one approach to enhance crop diversity whilst still keeping the integrity of a harvest rotation schedule. Many smaller types are available which are specially suited to container growing. Half-barrel planters are best for potatoes and berries and may be implanted in the following years with unrelated plants while the nightshades receive a twist in the raised beds.

Fertilizing and keeping your crops tomatoes are generally heavy-feeding plants. They like a soil full of organic matter and compost, but they also react well to side-dressing with fertilizers during the growing season. Maintaining suitable hydration is also crucial for creating the best berries. I explain all you want to understand in the subsequent sections.

Side-dressing - Side-dressing is incorporating a little bit of fertilizer around or even "on the side"

of crops once they're growing. Side-dress using a complete organic fertilizer, for example 5-5-5, is achieved by sprinkling a little handful of those fertilizer around each plant. Use the initial side-dressing when the tomatoes are golf-ball sized, then use another side-dressing each 3 months after that. Scratch the granular fertilizer to the top few inches of dirt. Use fertilizers with lesser levels of nitrogen; greater prices induce tomato plants to match a lot of leaves that are green and create few berries. Additionally, try not to find any fertilizer on the foliage; it may burn the leaves. If you would like to spray on your plants, treat your berries into some foliar feeding by mixing the fertilizer with water then spraying it on the plant leaves; this really can be a fast way to get nourishment into your plants. Employing fish emulsion or seaweed blend, dissolve the fertilizers in line with the recommendations on the bottle and spray on the plants every 3 months. Plants may take up nutrients quicker through their leaves than through their roots, but the effects do not last so long. Some research indicates that spraying plants with a seaweed mix may also decrease foliage diseases.

Tomatoes also enjoy Epsom salts. Studies have proven that 1 tablespoon of Epsom salts dissolved in 1 gallon of water and sprayed the transplant following planting and a month afterwards makes for healthier and more effective tomatoes.

Watering and mulching -Watering is critical if you would like your berries to create the highest quality fruits. Generally, berries need 1 inch of water weekly, but they might need longer in areas with warm, dry, windy summers. Among the greatest things you can do to conserve moisture would be to mulch around your tomato plants. Plastic mulch can conserve moisture but is best utilized along with soaker hoses or even the ditch watering approach. The very best water-conservation mulch is a 4- to 6-inch layer of hay. The mulch is thick enough to stop weeds from germinating and prevent the soil to dry off.

Straw mulches and hay keep soil cool, but berries love warmth. Therefore, if you are in a place that has cool summers, it's recommended to wait until the soil has heated and the crops are flourishing before mulching with all these substances. Mulching and watering equally may prevent many fruit issues, such as blossom-end rust and fruit freezing. See

the section "Weather-related Troubles" Later in
this chapter for information on such ailments.

ELIMINATING PESTS AND OTHER ISSUES

Tomatoes grow so vigorously they frequently outgrow any issues and give you a crop. However, to get the maximum from your crops, watch out for the problems in the subsequent segments, which are brought on by pests, diseases, or even weather. For an overall description of a strategy of activity against ordinary insects and diseases, spray pesticides only as a last resort; lots of crops can withstand a little infestation of insects or a couple of diseased leaves. Insects to watch for here are a couple of insects which are a specific problem with berries:

✓ Tomato hornworm: All these enormous, green caterpillars, which can develop up to 4 inches long, seem like the creature that ate Tokyo. They eat fruits and leaves of berries, and I swear that if you are quiet enough, you can hear them chewing gum. A couple of hungry hornworms can devastate a tomato plant immediately.

✓ Tomato Fruitworm: This green, 1-inch-long caterpillar with yellow or white stripes feeds on fruits and foliage. They may be handpicked from crops as with all the hornworm;

nonetheless, for a serious infestation, you can also spray crops with Bt.

√ Stink Bug: An issue mostly in warmer regions, these 1/2-inch-long grey or reddish shield-shaped insects primarily feed on fruits, inducing tough, white, or yellowish spots on the tomato skin. To control stink bugs, maintain your garden weed-free -- the insects hide in weeds across the garden -- and spray crops with pyrethrin.

Diseases:

√ Blights and leaf stains: The devastation begins with the reduced leaves becoming brown spots, turning yellowish, and finally dying. The signs of leaf spot seem like the indicators of early and late blight. The disease gradually spreads onto the plant, finally defoliating the entire plant. These bacterial infections are especially active during hot, wet weather. To restrain blight and leaf areas:

- Destroy and clean up all diseased foliage in the collapse.
- Rotate plants
- Mulch the plants with vinyl, hay, or straw after planting to prevent water from

round the spores out of the floor on the leaves.

- Before the illness becomes intense, spray with a natural fungicide, like aluminum or Bacillus subtilis.

✓ Verticillium And Fusarium Wilt: All these soil-borne fungal infections cause yellowing, wilting, and premature death of edible plants. Once contaminated, the crops will probably die and need to be taken off. The idea for prevention is to rotate your plantings and plant wilt-resistant plants (suggested by the letters F and V following the number name).

WEATHER-RELATED ISSUES

Not all issues with berries are linked to diseases or insects. Too much or too little fertilizer, too much water, chilly temperatures, and varietal differences can contribute to deformed fruits. Listed below are a couple of the common issues and some answers:

✓ Blossom Fall: Your berries are flowering superbly, but the blossoms all appear to fall without forming any fruit. This illness, known as blossom fall, results from air temperatures over 90 degrees Fahrenheit or below 55 degrees Fahrenheit. At these temperatures, most tomato blossoms won't place veggies. The remedy would be to develop varieties adapted to warmth (like 'Solar Fire') or cold weather (like 'Cold Set'). Or you may shield the plants during flowering with floating row covers.

✓ Blossom-End Rot: During this illness, the underside, or blossom end, of berries turns brownish and rots. Blossom-end rot is due to varying moisture conditions from the dirt, so the very best cure would be to mulch the plants nicely, plant them in well-drained dirt, and keep them.

✓ Fruit Cracking: several kinds of fruit cracking affect berries, but involve changing moisture conditions and vulnerability to cold temperatures early in this season. To avert this issue, plant varieties that are not as likely to decode (like 'Big Beef'), decrease nitrogen deposition, mulch the plants to maintain the soil moisture and shield flowering plants out of chilly nights with row covers.

- Sunscald: You will understand your berries have to sunscald in the event the best surfaces of the fruit skins have gently colored stains. These spots, which are brought on by direct exposure to sunlight, eventually rust. To steer clear of sunscald, develop indeterminate types that have a great deal of foliage to color the fruits (like 'Better Boy'), prevent pruning the leaves, and supply afternoon shade with colorful fabrics. Or you may grow the plants instead of staking them.

HARVESTING BERRIES

Harvest tomatoes when they are completely colored and compact to the touch. Tomatoes do not require direct sunlight to ripen, only warm temperatures. Tomatoes will last to ripen inside if they are chosen too early, therefore it is far better to err on the first side when picking. Provided that they show some color when chosen, they will ripen inside with that vine-ripened taste. If you would like to push the crop combined, you are able to prune off some fresh branches and small veggies to divert the plant's energy into the bigger fruits. You are also able to root-prune the plant, cutting 6 inches into the ground in a circle one foot off from the stem of this plant. Root-pruning severs a number of those roots, shocking the plant and forcing it to ripen its fruits quicker. It will, but block the creation of fresh fruits, therefore this technique is used towards the end of the season. If you reside in a place with bright sunshine, do not prune off tomato foliage. Eliminating too much foliage ends in sunscald, a state where the tomato skin actually gets sunburned. Sunscald itself does not destroy the tomato harvest, but it also opens the door to additional corrosion organisms to attack the fruit.

PEPPER AND EGGPLANTS

Peppers and eggplants, that can be just two tomato relatives (they are all at the nightshade, or Solanaceae, family), might not have the recognition of the large, red tomato cousins, however, their types have a comparable diversity of tastes, colors, and shapes. Peppers particularly are undergoing a resurgence of attention, and breeders have reacted to this interest by making new and improved types. Whether they're hot or sweet peppers, then you've got lots of new varieties to pick from. No longer just yellow, green, or red, sweet pepper forms come in a rainbow of colors, such as purple, orange, and chocolate. The newest types adapt better to hot and cold temperatures and possess more decorative attributes. With the prevalence of supper (which is currently the number-one condiment from the USA, as stated by the U.S. government), nachos, and hot foods generally, hot peppers have been gaining lots of focus too. In the mildest jalapeño into the newest 5-alarm habanero, varieties are offered for all taste buds and heat tolerances.

Eggplants (termed because some varieties have fruited the form and color of cows' eggs) are not as hot as carbohydrates, but they've gained a great deal of attention due to the discovery of types aside from the conventional dark purple, teardrop form. Long, lean, oriental kinds create superb grilled snacks, skin, and all. Small, round, green, Asian eggplants are excellent in soups and casseroles. You may even find unusual around, orange, Turkish kinds which are employed in specialty cultural cooking.

Both peppers and eggplants are amazing plants to grow in the garden, and they make excellent container plants when you have little space. Some grape types have purple stems, leaves, and fruits; eggplants have lovely purple blossoms, and the fruits may be many different colors, such as purple, white, gray-green, and orange. So, book a place in the vegetable or flower garden for all these gorgeous, edible fruits.

Selecting Some Hot Peppers To Grow:

Here are some hot pepper types which you're able to grow:

√'Anaheim TMR 23': These reasonably pungent, open-pollinated, smooth-skinned, 7-inch-long-by-2-inch-wide peppers are created on 3-foot-tall, leafy, tobacco mosaic virus-resistant (TMR) plants. They grow in 75 days. You may use the dried pods to produce the ristras (wreaths of dried peppers) popular in the Southwest.

√'Ancho 211' (Poblano): All these open-pollinated, reddish, somewhat hot, 4-inchlong, wrinkled, heart-shaped peppers frequently are filled and served as chile Rellenos. You are also able to wash them and make them into wreaths or powder. They just take 80 days to grow.

√'Large Chili II': This hybrid Anaheim-type roasting pepper is 8. To ten inches and mildly pungent. Yields are high and ancient in 68 days.

√'Cherry Bomb': All these somewhat sexy, 2-inch-round, thick-walled Hybrid fruits grow in 65 days into a glowing crimson.

√'Habanero' (Capsicum chinense): These are a few of the hottest peppers known to humanity! All these 1-inch-by-1-inch, lantern-shaped fruits grow to orange on 3-foot-tall open-pollinated plants. They flourish in the hot weather and also require a very long season to grow -- 100 days. The most popular range of the sort is a red variety called "Caribbean Red" which tops 445,000 about the Scoville scale.

These hot peppers may be harmful, so take caution when handling and ingesting them.

√'Hungarian Hot Wax': All these medium-hot, 7- to 8-inch-long, tapered open-pollinated peppers older from yellow to reddish and are fantastic for pickling. They just take 70 days to grow.

√ 'Jalapeño M': The traditional salsa, nacho, and pizza hot peppers. These reasonably hot, 3-inch-long, round-tipped open-pollinated fruits taste good when eaten red or green. 'Jalapa' is a much more productive hybrid variant, also 'Tam Jalapeño' is a milder selection. These peppers require 75 days to grow.

√ 'Mariachi': This AAS-winning hybrid pepper includes large returns of 4-inch-long and 2-inch-wide light fruits which are extremely attractive. The peppers begin yellowishly and grow into red in 66 days.

√'NuMex Joe E. Parker': An incredibly productive open-pollinated number of a favorite breeding line from New Mexico State University. The 6- to 7-inch long veggies possess a moderate to moderate spice. They grow in 65 days.

√'Serrano del Sol': All these candle-flame-shaped, 3 1/2-inch-long, Hot peppers have been created abundantly on 3-foot-tall plants. This new hybrid variant matures two weeks before and is more effective than the first "Serrano". With exactly the identical warmth as jalapeños, they are excellent in salsa and frequently are used in sauces. They grow in 64 days.

√'Super Cayenne III': These three to four-inch-long, fiery hot hybrid fruits taste good when consumed green or at adult red. The plants that are attractive are two feet tall and look great in containers. These peppers require 75 days to grow. An identical yellow-fruited variety known as "Yellow Cayenne" can be offered.

√ 'Thai Hot': All these 1-inch-long, fiery hot peppers out of Thailand mature in 80 days.

Ranked 1 and 1/2-foot-tall open-pollinated plants endure a lot of fruit, which makes them attractive ornamentals too. You are also able to try different varieties of pepper, such as 'Giant Thai Hot', which generates larger-sized fruit.

✓'Savory Habanero': 'This open-pollinated, first-ever mild habanero Pepper Requires only 100 on the Scoville scale. Red fruits are made abundantly within 90 days. You are able to definitely eat them from your hand!

A Couple of Tips for Starting and Planting:

Peppers and eggplants are warm-season plants, So you do not have to hurry to plant them before the earth has warmed up sufficiently. Here are some tips you can follow

✓ In many regions, you have to plant peppers and eggplants from seed inside, normally 6 to 8 weeks before the final frost date for your area. You are also able to buy them by a local nursery or via email as transplants.

✓ In case you live in zone 9 or 10, you can sow the seeds straight to your garden. Should you keep the plants healthy and don't have any frost in the area, peppers and eggplants can be perennials (plants that develop yearlong) and can bear fruit throughout the season.

But in cold climates, I have dug up pepper plants and eggplants in autumn, placed them in my greenhouse all winter, then transplanted them out in spring. Even after three decades these crops stay healthy and active. Peppers and eggplants are more finicky than berries are about temperatures, fertilization, and overall growing conditions, so they are less forgiving of errors. Thus, you have to take caution about beginning pepper and eggplant seedlings early inside. Give them ample dirt and water; harden off them nicely; then wait to plant when the soil temperature is at 60F. You need to buy or have raised a 4 to 6-inch tall, dark-green-leafed, stocky transplant which is not root-bound (roots growing around the container).

One handy product you might want to buy is a parasite. Normally costing less than $20, a soil thermometer can help you gauge when to plant warm-season crops like peppers and eggplants. Put it in a shady location and take readings in the morning for precision. In case your berries have flowered or place fruits until you have transplanted them when the seedlings have just four to six leaves remove any fruits or blossoms. The crops will then send more power to grow longer leaves and roots to encourage a bigger crop afterward instead of maturing just a few clicks ancient. Peppers and eggplants grow best in beds that are raised since the soil warms quicker and drains faster. These guidelines can help you get the dirt temperature right depending on your climate:

✓Cold places: Cover the top of the beds in case your peppers have flowered or place fruits until you have transplanted them when the seedlings have just four to six leaves remove any fruits or blossoms. The crops will then send additional energy to grow more leaves and roots to encourage a bigger harvest afterward instead of maturing just a few clicks ancient. Peppers and eggplants grow best in beds that are raised since the soil warms quicker and drains faster.

✓ Warm places: Mulch with straw, white vinyl, or aluminum foil in the summer to keep the soil cool. Aluminum foil also reflects light into the skies, perplexing insects seeking to discover plants. To plant pepper transplants and eggplant, use scissors to cut holes in the plastic mulch each 1 to 2 11/2ft (wider for taller types) for peppers and each 2 to 3ft for eggplants. If you are using mulch which is not plastic, plant in the very same distances as you want in plastic mulch. Plant eggplant and pepper transplant in precisely the exact same soil level as they are inside their containers. Cover the plantings using a floating row cover such as a lightweight, cheesecloth-like substance that allows water, air, and sun through to maintain the atmosphere warm and germs out.

Though pepper and eggplant crops are usually powerful enough to stand by themselves with supports, I like to stake or cage tall, heavy-yielding varieties like 'Carmen' and 'Black Beauty'. Staking or caging the crops retains fruits off the floor, making them less inclined to rust during moist weather. I discover I get milder yields this way too. Use small bets or tomato cages to maintain your crops vertical

Fertilizing and watering suggestions

Eggplants and peppers are sensitive to excessive fertilizer, particularly nitrogen. Plants fertilized with too much nitrogen will develop big but have few veggies. But don't neglect to prune your crops; just avoid using high levels of nitrogen fertilizers. Rather, apply a 2 to 3inch layer of compost over the bed and also a tiny number of 5-5-5 organic compost around every transplant. Watering is especially important through 90-degree weather when water pressure and high temperatures may cause blossoms to fall. Side-dress (insert fertilizer around the plants throughout the growing period) around the drip line (where water obviously drips off the ends of leaves) of this plant using a tbsp of fertilizer, for example 5-5-5. To present your peppers a grow, combine 1 tablespoon of Epsom salts in 1 gallon of water and spray on the pepper plants whenever they are flowering.

Pest patrol

You may see holes on a pepper fruit and you may locate a little, white egg within the fruit. The adult fly usually lays eggs on the fruit in midsummer. After the eggs hatch, the larvae then tunnel into the fruit. To control these insects, do the following:

✓ Rotate crops

✓ Cover youthful plants with row covers

✓ Grow types like 'Serrano' and 'Jalapeño' which are less appealing to the maggots

✓ Hang yellow sticky traps prior to the raised up gently lay eggs. Remove rotten fruits which will harbor the flies until you hang on the traps. Peppers and eggplants normally have fewer insect problems than their own tomato cousins, however, they discuss such diseases and pests because blossom fall, sunscald, blossom-end rot, fruit worms (also referred to as corn earworms), and Verticillium wilt.

Harvesting Tips

Peppers and eggplants are excellent to develop as you don't need to wait till the veggies are fully mature before you select them. Consider your choices for both veggies:

✓ Peppers: You're able to select and revel in sweet peppers or wait till they ripen to yellow, orange, or reddish for a sweeter flavor. Spicy peppers change in their hotness based on stress. Stressed peppers are somewhat milder, so in the event that you withhold fertilizer and water once the hot peppers have been ripening, you can boost the warmth in the peppers' taste. Cool, cloudy weather will create hot peppers.

✓ Eggplants: You are able to select eggplants in just about any stage. The key is not to let them become over-mature; differently they will get soft and mushy. To test eggplant maturity, see the fruit's skin. A dull-colored skin means it is overly mature. Double-check by clipping to the fruit and taking a look at the seeds. Brown-colored seeds are just another indication of over adulthood. An easy test for maturity will be to push the eggplant's skin with your fingernail. If the skin bounces back, the veggies are ready to harvest. If your nail indents skin, The veggies are over mature. If your veggies are really older and rotting on the vine, just select them and toss them out; they will not taste really good. The key to harvesting would be to do it frequently. The more frequently you crop, the sweeter the eggplants you're getting. To harvest, cut peppers and eggplants using a sharp knife just over the surface of the green cap onto the fruit. The fruits will last to ripen once you harvest them so keep them in a cool location. If you would like to dry your peppers, select them when they grow and hang them to dry in a living area with good airflow.

SELECTING YOUR ONION VARIETIES

From the following lists of my favorite onion types, I differentiate between onions which are long day, short day, and intermediate afternoon (or day impartial). Within each class are pungent and sweet varieties. These kinds are the most frequently adapted (able to develop in a huge array of geographical areas under different weather conditions) and also easiest to grow. Bear in mind that pungent onions are a lot better for storage compared to sweet varieties. I also suggest whether you're able to buy the variety for a set (small onions which were praised so they grow quicker) or as one plant. The days to maturity are from directly seeding from the garden or setting out (putting outdoors) plants or sets. Short-day onions are usually planted in autumn to rise throughout the winter so that they take longer to mature than other forms. Extended and intermediate day blossoms are often implanted in spring. Each of the blossoms have yellowish skin and white flesh unless otherwise noticed.

Short-day onions feature the following varieties:

✓'Giant Red Hamburger': This open-pollinated, sweet, short-day variety features dark reddish skin and red and white flesh. It evolves in 95 days from seeding and may be bought as a plant.

✓'Granex 33' (Vidalia): This classic hybrid onion is a renowned short-day selection. It's accessible as a plant also is famous in the Southeast. It evolves in spring, 180 days following fall seeding.

✓'Texas Grano 1015' (Texas Super candy): This sweet, short-day hybrid can grow as big as a baseball and remain sweet. Additionally, it is available as a plant and it also is currently popular in Texas and in the Southwest. It evolves 175 days from seeding.

Intermediate-day (or even day-neutral) onion types include the following:

✓'Candy': This sweet, hybrid, intermediate-day onion is broadly adapted. Additionally, it is available as a plant. It hastens 85 days following seeding.

✓'Italian Red Torpedo': This sweet, Italian heirloom, intermediate-day, red onion strains a bottle-shaped bulb with a mild flavor and pink flesh. It hastens 110 days following seeding.

✓ 'Superstar': This all-american selections winning, hybrid, white-skinned, sweet onion generates a 1-pound, disease-resistant, uniform, mild-tasting bulb 109 times from planting. It is isn't great for long-term storage due to its sweetness.

Long-day onion types include the following:

✓'Ailsa Craig Exhibition': This yellow-skinned, open-pollinated variety is famous for its sweet flavor, it can grow 2-pound bulbs after 105 days following seeding. It tolerates cool weather nicely.

✓'Borrettana cipollini': Cipollini are an exceptional Italian, flat-shaped varieties. The 'Borrettana' variety produces 2-inch-diameter yellow sweet onions which are good braided and great caramelized and sautéed. It hastens 110 days following seeding. 'Red Marble' is a fantastic reddish cipollini type variety.

✓ 'Copra': It is possible to keep this hybrid, pungent variety until spring. It hastens 104 days following seeding.

✓ 'Purple': This purple-skinned mini-onion is best harvested when 3 to 4 inches in diameter 60 days following seeding. It's gentle, sweet pink flesh and really is a great one for pickling. Additionally, it may be utilized as a scallion.

✓'Yellow Sweet Sandwich': This hybrid actually gets sweeter in storage, and it also comes as a white-skinned variant referred to as 'White Sweet Sandwich'. Both versions can be found as plants. The number matures 100 days following seeding.

✓'Walla Walla Sweet': This sweet hybrid has light yellow color and great cold tolerance. It is available as a plant that is famous in the Northwest. It hastens 115 days following seeding.

✓'Yellow Stuttgarter': This pungent, regular, open-pollinated storage variety frequently is marketed as a place. It matures in approximately 90 times from a group and 120 days following seeding.

Looking at scallions and continuing onions

You might have run across several other onion kinds in restaurants or create markets. By way of instance, scallions (also known as bunching onions, spring onions, or green onions) are chosen due to their delicate, succulent, green shirts until they shape bulbs. Scallions occupy less space on your garden than normal onions since it's possible to plant them closer together, and they are able to provide you a fast harvest when planted in autumn or spring. Growing scallions is a fantastic way for beginner onion growers to get started. Any onion variety developed out of a seed can be chosen as a scallion, however here several varieties which are especially broadly adapted as scallions:

✓ 'Evergreen Hardy White': This hardy, white-stalked variety is an excellent alternative for cold climates (USDA zone 5), and it may overwinter if secure and utilized as a perennial. It hastens 65 days following seeding.

✓'Red Beard' (*Allium fistulosum*): This tender species has special coloring: a reddish stem using a white tip and leaves. It hastens 45 days following seeding.

✓ 'White Spear': This heat-resistant scallion features thick white stalks and blue-green leaves. Great for warm climates. It hastens 65 days following seeding. Multiplier or perennial, onions return year after year and replicate easily. Here are the two chief kinds:

✓ Egyptian top-set blossoms (also called Walking or shrub onions): All these blossoms reproduce by forming clusters of onion collections on the ends of their rising stalks, as shown in Figure 6-1. Since the weight pulls down the stalks, the root of the cluster where they land, which makes the blossoms seem as though they're walking slowly throughout your garden. Throughout winter, Egyptian top-set blossoms mainly are consumed as scallions, but the top-sets create great, little, sweet onions once you select them. They are also rather a cold hardy.

✓ Potato onions: All these onions form a primary onion from a fall planting. They are tough to USDA zone 4 and also create many smaller collections which it is possible to replant following summer harvest to generate more onions the subsequent calendar year.

POTATOES: NO LONGER A BORING SPUD

When I had to vote the most underrated vegetable on the planet, I'd decide on the potato (Solanum tuberosum). Potatoes have a reputation for being ordinary, widely accessible, cheap, and only plain brownish and dull. So why bother growing them? Well, to start with, the taste and feel of fresh potatoes dug in the ground is far better than the bagged spuds that sit grocery-store shelves for months. It is also enjoyable to develop several distinct varieties, such as novelty potatoes like purple, red, or yellow types. You will surely astound your loved ones and dinner guests with those, not so-plain potatoes. Potatoes are one of the most foolproof plants to grow. Start planting early, although the weather remains cool, by putting a bit of this tuber (known as a seed potato) at a furrow, or trench. Following the potatoes begin growing, should you hill them (push the dirt around the plants), water them and keep away the bugs, you are almost guaranteed some fantastic tubers. I describe more about planting berries and supply hints on developing sweet potatoes, a distinctive sort of root harvest.

Selecting a Couple of curry varieties

So many potato varieties can be found that narrowing the area is often hard. But you might choose to try out some of my favorites, which I explain in the next listing. I have included some fingerling types which are the newest rage; they create plenty of small tubers that are good roasted, grilled, or steamed. Here are my favorite potato varieties depending on taste, color, and simplicity of growth:

✓ 'All Blue': This mid- to late-season spud has blue skin and flesh. It's a mealy texture, so it is better as a mashed potato. Yes, blue mashed potatoes! You are also able to develop a comparable 'All Red' (known as 'Cranberry Red') variety that's reddish skin on the outside and pink flesh in the interior. Coupled with 'All Blue' potatoes plus a white selection, you may produce a red, white, and blue mashed potato extravaganza!

✓'Butte': This late-season variety is your timeless Idaho baking potato. It is an excellent russeted (contains rough, brown-colored epidermis) baking variety which contains 20% more protein and 58% more vitamin C than other types. Additionally, it is tolerant of scab disease and late blight.

✓'Caribe': This ancient, lavender-skinned, white-fleshed variety creates large tubers. A fantastic masher.

✓ 'Kennebec': This all-purpose midseason range with white flesh and skin is reliable, resists disease, also so is very good for just about any use.

✓ 'King Harry': This early-season, white-fleshed and gold-skinned and gold-skinned and variety is exceptional because of its hairy leaves which allegedly ward off insects, like Colorado potato beetles, leafhoppers, and flea beetles. Oh, and also the spuds taste great, too!

✓ 'Red Norland': This ancient variety has red skin and white flesh. Harvested early when crops are only flowering, this number is often sold in markets as a fresh red potato. It tastes best boiled or mashed.

✓'Rose Finn Apple': This late-maturing fingerling variety Features raised colored skin and yellow flesh. It's a firm, moist texture and can be great boiled or baked.

CLASSIFYING CARROTS BY FORM

Carrots frequently are called a particular kind, like baby carrots. Table 6-1 shows the typical kinds of carrots as well as their characteristics. Each of the types recorded, except baby carrots and imperators, vary in size from 6 to 8 inches. Besides the fact that eating carrots is refreshing, you may also best utilize specific types for juicing and saving; a few even grow well in containers.

Assessing Some Carrot Varieties

Knowing what sort of carrot a particular selection is can assist you when deciding which type to grow. With a few of the most frequently known carrot kinds, you can readily recognize the carrot kind since it is a part of this variety's title; a few examples comprise 'Scarlet Nantes' and 'Danvers 126'. Otherwise, you just read the description to learn. They also have particular features that will make them ideal for your garden; they are tasty, disease-resistant, and easy to grow. All are great for baking. The times to maturity are from seeding from the floor until first crop. Nonetheless, early-season carrot types are yummy even when you harvest them before they fully mature:

✓ 'Atomic Red': This imperator-type, open-pollinated carrot possesses 9-inch-long roots that are reddish from the skin to center. The color deepens and the taste gets lighter when cooked. This variety matures in 70 days.

✓ 'Bolero': This hybrid vehicle, Nantes-type lettuce generates 6-inch-long roots and 8135*contains additional disease resistance and shops nicely. It evolves in 72 days. 'Yaya' is a more recent hybrid variety that is sweeter and matures earlier (60 times) compared to 'Bolero'.

✓'Danvers 126': All these heat-resistant, open-pollinated roots produce significant yields of 7to 8-inch-long carrots 70 days after planting.

✓'Health master': " This hybrid vehicle, Danvers-type number grows up to 10 inches long and comprises 30 percent more vitamin A compared to other lettuce kinds. It matures in 110 days.

✓ 'Kuroda': This hybrid vehicle, 6-inch-long, Chantenay-type produces heavy yields of carrots that are beneficial for juicing and keeping. It evolves in 79 days.

✓'Little Finger': " This open-pollinated variety is an early (65 Times), 3-inch long, smooth-skinned, small-cored infant lettuce that is sweet. 'Little Finger' carrots are fantastic for planting containers.

✓ 'Merida': This hybrid, Nantes-type, 7- to 8-inch-long carrot may be planted in spring for fall harvest. But it is most likely raised as a fall crop and in mild-winter locations, like the Pacific Northwest, in which it could overwinter (live through winter) and be chosen in spring. It evolves in 75 days.

✓ 'Parmex': This hybrid vehicle, baby-type carrot features 1 1⁄2-inch-diameter round roots which are chosen in 50 days. Perfect for planting in shallow reefs.

✓'Purple Haze': This hybrid vehicle, 10- to 12-inch-long Imperator Has purple skin and an orange heart. This candy variety's purple color fades when cooked. It evolves in 70 days.

✓'Scarlet Nantes': This heirloom, Nantes-type assortment has bright Red-orange flesh which has a little core. The 6- to 7-inch-long roots older in 65 days.

✓'Short Pants Sweet': This 4-inch, open-pollinated, Chantenay-type carrot grows well in heavy clay soil and containers. It evolves in 68 days.

✓ 'Sugarsnax': This hybrid vehicle, Imperator-type number is as sweet and tender as a Nantes number, yet it grows around 9 inches, is disease resistant, and is full of beta carotene. It evolves in 68 days.

✓ 'Thumbelina': This odd hybrid, baby-type, All-America Selections winner includes a round root that is the duration of a silver dollar; it is particularly great for baking. It grows well in containers and into thick soil or rocky land. It evolves in 65 days. Children love this variety because of its small dimensions and easy-growing character.

√'White Satin': This hybrid vehicle, Nantes and Imperator cross Includes 8-inchlong crisp, textured white branches that grow under a wide selection of weather and soil conditions. It evolves in 68 days.

CHAPTER 5 - GROWING AND FIXING ROOT CROPS: THE BEST PLANT TO GROW

Root plants are easy to grow when you've got good soil, water, and appropriate spacing. The puzzle of root plants is that you cannot find the reward until you dig up. Nonetheless, that is half of the fun of developing them.

GENERAL STRATEGIES FOR YOUR ROOT CROPS

The key to developing good root crops is organizing the soil bed nicely and giving the plants room to grow. Also, you will need to keep the plants clear of weeds and be certain that they have sufficient water. Here are additional details on all the important points:

✓ All root crops want loose, fertile soil. Except for tomatoes that grow best in mountains, root plants grow best in raised beds. They can also grow when you've got a gardening place that has just 4 to 6 hours of sunlight every day. Try out some onions and carrots in that spot.

To prepare the soil, add a three to four inch layer of compost or mulch at least two to three weeks until you are ready to plant. Should you wait until just before planting to include new mulch, then you are very likely to find bad development. Why? Too much nitrogen fertilizer carrots and potatoes in spring boost foliage growth but maybe not superior tuber and root formation. Rather, root plants like phosphorous promote root development, so carry out a soil test, include a bone meal or rock phosphate fertilizer before planting to maintain your roots contented. Onions specifically like plenty of fertilizer, and they can endure a little excess nitrogen, which promotes leaf development. Insert additional fertilizer once the transplants are 6 inches tall and the bulbs start to swell. Add an entire organic fertilizer, for example 5-5-5, at 1 lb every 10 feet.

Root plants, especially onions and carrots, require appropriate spacing to grow to their potential. Thin out the young seedlings when they are 3 to 4 months old by yanking them out or snipping them till they are properly spaced. Onions ought to be 4 inches apart, scallions 2 inches apart, and carrots 3 inches apart. Potatoes do not need thinning and need to be planted 8 to 10 inches apart. I am aware that thinning your heavy plants seems unkind, but if you do not do it, the roots will not have sufficient space to enlarge, causing one to get a lot of crops but few follicles -- and fewer follicles imply fewer onions and carrots.

✓ You will be rewarded with plenty of crisp roots in no time if you regularly bud your root harvest patch. After a great thinning, hand-weed bed of onions and carrots; berries can be weeded using a hoe. Mulch the bed with straw or hay. You do not need to mulch in-between carrot and onion plants. Then you have to mulch around the beds, and keep them watered.

Onions, carrots, and potatoes are root plants that enjoy cooler temperatures. They develop best and have the best taste when temperatures remain below 80 degrees Fahrenheit.

Cultivating carrots

Carrot seeds are small and take around two weeks to germinate, which means you run a much greater chance of poor germination together than with other veggies. To receive your carrots off to the ideal foot, try these hints:

✓ Prevent forked roots in carrots by making sure that the soil doesn't have any stones, sticks, and tough parts of soil. If the carrot roots come in contact with a hard thing when they're growing, they fork, developing a multipronged carrot. Though they're fascinating to check at along with a conversation piece, forked roots are more difficult to wash and give fewer carrots. No dirt could be wholly free of sticks and rocks, but when constructing a raised bed try to eradicate as many as you can. And make sure you amend the soil with compost to generate the soil looser so that the roots remain straight. If your soil is heavy clay or even a stone jungle, then consider growing round varieties like 'Thumbelina'.

✓ For simpler germination of little carrot seeds, consider buying pelleted seeds. These seeds have been coated with a biodegradable coating, which makes the seed bigger and easier to deal with. On the other hand, seed germination is not affected. Sprinkle carrot seeds onto the cover of the ground and cover them with a thin layer of potting soil or sand. Potting soil and sand tend to be milder compared to garden soil, allowing tender tails to easily grow through.

✓ Maintain your soil moisture. If it dries, then the seedlings can easily perish.

✓ Grow them as a fall harvest, beginning 1 to 2 weeks before your first frost. They germinate quicker in the warmer land summertime, and their taste is sweeter when they grow in cooler autumn weather. In hot summer areas, you might have to color your freshly sown soil using a color cloth; warm soil temperatures interfere with proper seed germination.

In case your carrot tops break off throughout crop (some do), use a garden fork to dig their roots. Pull the most significant carrot roots to leave space for the bigger roots to complete. And if you can not eat all of your carrots until the first freeze, then place a 6 to 8inch-thick layer of hay over the carrot bed. This layer of security is going to continue to keep the soil thawed, letting you head on a winter's day and harvest new carrots directly until spring. If you are hungry for carrots and can not wait 'til they completely grow, you can harvest youthful carrots anytime after the roots have formed. They simply will not taste as sweet if you don't develop the infant kinds.

ORGANIZING YOUR ROWS WITH BEAN FAMILY PLANTS

All bush, stick, and dried beans are members of the Fabaceae family. Within this part, I categorize beans depending on their growth habits and use (in other words, if you eat them fresh or dried). Here are the groups:

✓ Bush legumes: These beans get their name because they grow to a bush. They tend to generate the oldest plants, maturing all at once (in just a week or so of every other); you've either feast or famine with those kinds.

✓ Pole legumes: These legumes require staking and generally grow on sticks. They tend to grow their plants later than bush beans, however, stick beans continue to create all season until disease or frost stops them. (Fortunately, home gardeners don't need to be concerned about disease resistance by using their bean plants)

✓ Dried legumes: All these are types of bush or pole beans. You may eat them fresh, such as bush or pole beans, but they are better if you let them dry and then simply eat the bean seeds. Growing dried beans is simple: Simply plant them, care for them and harvest them when the pods are dried and the crops are nearly dead.

Bush and stick beans really would be the same kind of bean, only with different growth habits. Bush and stick beans frequently are known as snap beans since they snap when you break their pods . Another name for those beans would be string beans, since ancient varieties needed a stringy texture. (Modern varieties do not have this feel, so this title is not commonly used now.) Yellow snap kinds mature into a yellowish color and are known as wax beans. Do not get lost in the snap versus series discussion. These are only names people have contributed to some bean consumed before the seeds indoors start to form. Beans chosen at various phases can be called different names. Think about the following:

√ A bean chosen when it is young, before seeds have shaped, is referred to as a snap bean. They are available in yellow, green, or purple depending upon the variety.

√ When a bean develops further and you crop it If it is still youthful but the bean seeds are fully formed, it is referred to as a shell bean.

✓ When the pod dries on the plant then you Harvest it, it is known as a dried bean

Bushels of Bush Beans

Bush bean crops normally are less than 2ft tall and create handfuls of beans in their main crop of the year. Based upon the number, the beans are yellow, green, or purple. Most pods (the component of the bean which you consume) are just 6 to 8 inches in maturity, however you can harvest beans which are yummy sooner. Should you want plenty of beans at the same time for canning or maintaining, develop bush beans. Selecting one of the several kinds is only an issue of color and experimentation; try one and see whether you prefer it. Listed below are a Couple of of the Most Dependable types to grow :

✓'Blue Lake 274': This large, meaty, green bean collection matures High yields (approximately 12 pounds for each 10 ft of row) within 55 times -- even under adverse weather conditions. Additionally, it comes at a pole bean variant.

✓ 'Derby': This disease-resistant green bean is a All-America Selections winner (see Chapter 4) and contains extra-tender pods and high yields 57 days to seeding.

✓'Improved Golden Wax': This disease-resistant, yellow-bean number Generates broad, horizontal golden pods 52 days from seeding.

✓ 'Jade': This heat-tolerant green bean generates huge yields of pencil straight legumes 60 days following seeding. It generates high quality beans into the season than other green grasses beans, enabling you to expand your harvest time.

✓'Kentucky Wonder': This classic green bean round, green pods Are produced prolifically on hardy plants 57 days from seeding. Additionally, it comes at a pole bean selection.

✓ 'Nash': This thick foliage, disease-resistant variety grows well in the heat, so it is a fantastic alternative in hot-summer places. Its green pods older 54 days from seeding.

✓ 'Provider': This number includes good disease resistance and may grow in unfavorable weather. Its green pods older 50 days from seeding.

✓'Roc d'Or Wax': This number produces long, slender, round, Bright yellow pods sturdy crops in 53 days.

✓ 'Roma II': This Romano-type noodle bean contains tender, flat pods and large yields sooner than Romano (53 days after seeding). The pods are slow to strings and develop seeds, so that they remain tender more.

✓ 'Romano': This long, horizontal green bean is also an Italian classic and comes at a rod variety. The pods are famous for their powerful taste and ability to keep tender even if they are large. This variety matures in 60 days. 'Romano Gold' and 'Romano Purpiat' are purple and yellow varieties, respectively, which grow like the first only with different-colored pods.

✓'Royal Burgundy': This alluring purple-podded bean also includes a Purple tinge on its leaves, stalks, and flowers. It matures in 55 times also turns dark green when cooked.

Pole Beans: The Long and Tall Crop

Many rod bean varieties talk about the titles and features that the bush bean presents. Pole beans grow more legumes overall but begin a week or so after than bush beans and create just a couple of beans every day, making them great for smaller families. Pole beans maintain generating beans until freeze, in all but the most popular summer locations. You are also able to plant them for a fall harvest in warm locations. Below I'm going to list the pole beans that also have bush types, and some other well-producing pole sorts:

√ 'Blue Lake': Watch the bush variety from the previous section.

√ 'Emerite': Think about the number as a green filet bean (see the subsequent section "Other legumes") on sticks. The tender, pencil-thin, 4 to 5inch-long pods have been made 64 days from seeding.

✓ 'Fortex': This variety creates extra-long (11-inch) pods which are stingless, tender, nutty, and salty. A French favored, this green bean pops 60 days from seeding.

✓ 'Goldmarie': This ancient yielding, wax rod bean collection generates 8inch pods 54 days from seeding.

✓'Kentucky Wonder': Watch the bush bean collection from the previous section for a description. 'Kentucky Wonder' also is offered in a wax rod bean variety.

✓ 'Purple Pod': This distinctive purple-colored variety develops to a 6 foot- all plant. If you cook the bean, its color changes from purple to dark green. It evolves 65 days from seeding.

✓ 'Romano': Watch the bush bean collection from the previous section.

✓ 'Scarlet Runner': This gorgeous, vigorous rod bean is really in another species compared to other pole beans (Phaseolus coccineus). It creates attractive scarlet red flowers, big hairy pods, and bean seeds which are edible 70 days from seeding. The pods could be eaten young and the bean seeds are edible when dried. This variety tastes fine, but it generally is raised as an ornamental because of its attractive flowers and vivid black and red bean seeds.

The Versatile Shell and Dried Beans

Shell and dried beans are a few of the most versatile beans to grow since you can eat them in the snap, shell, or even dried phases. Eaten in the shell point (completely cultivated seeds in the pod, however the exterior remains green) or dried point, you are eating the seed in the pod. These seeds come in colors from white to red and may even be spotted. Dried beans are excellent baked in soups and chowders. The majority of the types in the following list have been developed for their edible beans but taste great in their paychecks point, also. They are the dried beans which the majority of individuals are knowledgeable about eating, and they are the tastiest to develop. The times to maturity signify time from seeding to dried bean crop. The majority of these types are bushy plants:

✓ 'Black Turtle': This tiny black bean matures 85 days after seeding and develops best in warmer climates. Each pod generates seven to eight legumes, which are usually baked in addition to used in soups and casseroles.

✓'Blue Speckled Tepary': This Southwest variety develops great in dry conditions. The brown seeds with red speckles need 90 days from seeding.

✓ 'Cannellini': This famed white, kidney-shaped bean is frequently utilized in minestrone. Huge plants produce beans which are best when consumed in the shelling phase, which can be 80 times from seeding.

✓ 'French Horticultural': A long-time favorite, this tan-colored bean matures in 90 days. You are also able to consume this number sooner as a shelling bean.

✓'Jacob's Cattle': This bean receives its title from the cows that Jacob, the biblical personality, tended. It is white with splashes of maroon. This bean is best suited to cooler weather. You will find'Jacob's Cattle' good in baked bean dishes.

√ 'Navy': This little, semi-vining plant produces white, oval beans 85 days from seeding. These legumes are excellent .

√ 'Pinto': A vining plant generates buff-colored, brown-speckled, dried beans 90 days from seeding; those legumes are frequently utilized in Mexican dishes. You are also able to grow this variety for a pole bean.

√ 'Red Kidney': This bushy plant produces large, reddish, kidney-shaped legumes 100 days from seeding. These legumes are used in several delectable dishes. 'Red Kidney' also comes as a white-seeded selection.

√ 'Soldier': This white, kidney-shaped bean with reddish markers generates 6 beans per pod 85 days from seeding. This bean is excellent baked in stews.

√'Tongue of Fire': These six- to seven-inch, red-streaked pods could be eaten shelled or dried. They mature into the shell period 70 days from seeding.

√'Vermont Cranberry': This crimson, brown-speckled, New England classic dried bean is among the most well-known beans to grow. It evolves 90 days from seeding and can be broadly adapted (can develop in many different geographical areas below many different weather conditions).

Peas

One vegetable that is truly a cure to develop yourself is peas, which are also called Pisum sativum botanically. In grocery stores, peas are offered for just a brief while, and their taste is not as tender and sweet as lately harvested pea pods. Some types grow to be enormous and bushy, requiring additional support to stay tall. Others are short and don't require support or fencing. Viny pea plants create a grabbing shoot referred to as a tendril that retains onto anything it comes in touch with. Some publication types do not even bother growing leaves. In the subsequent sections, I split peas into three classes: English, Snap and Snow. Head your peas and have a peek at some excellent kinds. A pea is explained by the sort of pods it is in. Here are the groups:

✓ An English, or garden, pea includes a challenging pod with tender peas inside.

✓ A Snap pea has tender peas indoors but also an edible, sweet pod.

✓ A Snow pea is chosen (that can be harvested before the pea seeds within the pod shape) chiefly because of its tender pea pod.

English peas: The dependable standby

Sometimes known as the garden pea, the English pea is your pea that anglers are familiar with and that is most commonly raised. From the next listing, the times to maturity represent time from seeding to harvest. Here are a few of the most dependable varieties of English peas:

✓'Alderman' (Tall Telephone): This old heirloom develops in approximately 74 days. Six-foot-tall vines generate a lot of 4 to 5inch pods to 2 peas per gallon.

✓ 'Blondie': This new assortment includes 3inch long pods using 8 beans per gallon. The yellowish leaves and light green pods and peas make it eye-catching variety from the garden. It evolves in 65 days and requires trellising (that I discuss in the next section "Spacing correctly and supplying support").

✓ 'Feisty': This 30inch tall blossom includes few leaves and lots of tendrils, making the medium-sized pea pods to 8 beans per pod a lot easier to harvest. The plant matures in 61 days.

✓'Little Marvel': Although it is a dwarf plant which develops Just 18-20 inches high, this pea plant produces heavy yields of 3-inch pods using 6 to 2 peas per gallon. The plant matures in 62 days.

✓ 'Maestro': A successful early number matures in 60 days and reaches just two feet tall but generates 4- to 2 5-inch pods with 9 to 11 peas per gallon on powdery mildew resistant plants.

✓ 'Mr. Big': This All-America-Selections-winning, disease resistant variety is a huge manufacturer that develops in 67 days. The five- to six-foot tall vines produce 4 to 5inch long pods up to ten peas per gallon.

✓ 'Petit Pois': This book baby pea (the pea seed within the pod is much smaller compared to the standard pea seed) is extra tender and sweet. It generates 6 to seven peas per day. The crops are 20 inches tall and create snacks in 58 days.

✓ 'Wando': This very effective, hot weather variety grows 3 feet tall and produces 7 to 2 peas per gallon in 68 days.

Sweet and tender snap peas

Snap peas are the newest peas on the block. Today they've become a mainstay in many households. Snap pea pods (the pea seed within the pod types) such as a English pea, however they have a pleasant, tender pod such as a snow pea. Some newer types are deemed stingless. The plants vary in the first 'Super Snap' that grows to 2 feet tall into the diminutive 'Sugar Bon' that develops to less than two feet tall. Children love snap peas, and they are as easy to develop as English peas. Try out these kinds of candy and yummy snap peas:

✓ 'Cascadia': All these 2-foot-tall vines resist the pea enation virus disorder (an issue in the Pacific Northwest; visit the subsequent section "Pesky pea issues") and create 3-inch, dark green peas 58 days following planting.

✓ 'Sugar Ann': This is earliest maturing snap pea, this number is ready for harvest in 52 days. The plants grow just two feet tall, making sweet, 2 to 3inch pods. Since this snap pea is a dwarf selection, it does not require support and could be raised in containers. 'Sugar Sprint' is very similar to 'Sugar Ann' but does not create stringy pods.

✓ 'Sugar Bon': A 1 to 2foot tall snap pea, this plant develops in 56 days and resists powdery mildew disease. Due to its dimensions, this number is superb for containers.

✓'Sugar Lace II': All these 30-inch-tall vines have couple of leaves and Many tendrils, which makes the 3-inch-long pods simple to see. The plant is self-supporting and disease resistant. It evolves in 68 days.

'Super Sugar Snap': All these blossoms grow to 6 ft tall, making a lot of sweet, long pods and legumes 65 days after planting. This variety is briefer and much more disease resistant than the first 'Sugar Snap', which will be still offered.

Snow peas

If you have eaten a vegetable dish at a Chinese restaurant, you have likely tried these sweet-tasting, flat-podded peas. Snow peas are the simplest peas to grow since you don't need to await the pea pods to fill out to crop them. They are tender, stingless, and greatest if chosen before the peas inside start to swell. Here are a few of the best generating varieties to attempt:

✓'Dwarf Gray Sugar': This viny, 2 to 3foot tall plant demands support but generates 3inch, dark green pods 57 days following planting. The pink blossoms this plant generates are decorative, and that means you're going to enjoy how they dress your garden .

✓'Golden Sweet': This Indian heirloom features exceptional golden-colored pods 6foot tall green plantations that grow in 65 days. The pods remain golden when cooked, which makes them beautiful additions to stir-fry and fries.

✓'Mammoth Melting Sugar': " This 4 to 5foot tall heirloom features 5-inch long pods which remain sweet more than other types. It evolves in 68 days following planting.

✓'Oregon Giant': These big 4 to 5inch candies pods grow disease Resistant, 3foot tall vines 60 days following planting.

✓ 'Oregon Sugar Pod II': Another sweet-tasting snow pea with large-podded, this number grows to 4 feet tall and hastens its pods 68 days following planting. Much like 'Oregon Giant', it is also disease resistant.

CHAPTER 6 - PLANTING LEGUMES FOR AN EXTENSIVE HARVEST

When planting beans, select a sunny place with well-drained soil, and make a raised bed. Raised beds maintain pea seeds from becoming soggy while they float in cool spring dirt; in precisely the exact same time, raised beds warm up the dirt to bean seeds, which you plant from late spring and summertime. In the subsequent sections, I describe how to prepare the soil for the beans, find out when to plant, and then find out how to provide them the correct support. Plants need nitrogen to grow, and the majority of the time they get it from the ground. Legumes are exceptional; however, they also may use the nitrogen from the atmosphere via a particular relationship with a kind of bacteria known as a rhizobium. This germ normally occurs in soil and attaches itself into legume roots, living off plants. On the market, the germs take the atmospheric nitrogen and transform it into a form the plants can utilize. Beans and peas have the nitrogen they want, and the germs get a house. Therefore don't be concerned about adding more nitrogen fertilizer into beans; they could treat these. Should you see lumps or nodules on the roots of the crops, you understand that germs are at work.

These kinds of soil require a one-time inoculation (the mixing of powder seeds in planting), which carbohydrates the dirt with bacteria and provides plants the boost that they need. After this the rhizobium is in the dirt, so you do not have to include it annually. Though beans do not require additional nitrogen, they gain from a 2 to 3inch layer of composted manure worked into the soil prior to planting. For poor soils with low fertility, include a natural fertilizer high in potassium and phosphorous, for example 5-5-5.

DECIDING WHEN TO PLANT

With legumes, wait until the soil is at least 60 degrees Fahrenheit before planting. Beans planted in cool soil die before germinating. Stagger your bush bean planting dates by sowing little batches of seeds each week or so. By shocking the plantings, you will have a constant harvest during summer. Peas like soil; in actuality, they could germinate in 40-degree land. Whenever the soil dries out, assemble your raised beds and plant your seeds. You can decide whether your soil is dried out by squeezing a few, and if no water pops out and the dirt clump feels moist and breaks up easily when poked with your finger, then the soil is dried out. You can plant beans 3 to 4 months before the final frost date in your town if the dirt is prepared. Pea seeds germinate better at 60 to 70 degree dirt, but should you wait 'til the soil is warmer, then the crops will return to a late start. From the time that the peas will start flowering, the air temperature could be too hot (over 80 degrees), along with your plants and creation will endure. You are also able to develop peas as a fall harvest, which you begin in summer so the crops grow during the cool days of fall. I have had success planting snow beans as a fall harvest. It's possible to harvest these beans sooner than English and skillet since it is possible to eat the horizontal pea pods once they shape and until the freezing weather strikes. To assist pea seeds germinate in hot or cold lands, consider peregrinating the seeds. Put the pea seeds in a moist paper towel in a dark, warm place for a couple of days. Verify the seeds every day; once you find a little root start to grow, plant the beans in the floor. Peregrinating assists the beans get off to a quicker start and lowers the possibility they'll rust in cool dirt.

Spacing correctly and providing support

Just how near you plant your beans depends on the types you have chosen. These guidelines will help:

✓ Bush beans grow best in rows along with a raised bed. In rows one to two feet apart, plant the seeds in 1 to 2 inches of one another. Subsequently lean the beans to 6 inches apart once they germinate and emerge in the ground. (Chapter 13 provides pointers about how best to narrow your vegetable seedlings.)

✓ Since you plant peas once the dirt is cooler, the germination percentage could be less compared to legumes. So, in your bed, plant your peas less than 1 inch apart in rows 6 inches apart. Tall vining types of legumes, like pole beans, and tall types of peas require support to cultivate their very best. The kind of support required is dependent upon the plant. Pole bean shoots spiral and wrap themselves about items they can scale, and legumes attach themselves to items using tendrils (catching shoots which hold onto anything they are in contact). Normally, legumes like to grow sticks like to scale fences. The height of your fence or rod is dependent upon the varieties that you are growing: A 4 to 5foot fence is very good for many peas, along with a 6 to 8foot rod is fantastic for pole beans. Maintain your fences and poles inside reach since if the crops grow too tall, then you ought to use a ladder to crop. To learn more about trellises, fences, and teepees.

Thwarting Pests and Diseases

One nice thing about legumes and lentils is that they are vulnerable to just a couple of serious pests or diseases. But a number of the usual issues that plague other veggies, like damping off, fusarium wilt, powdery mildew, and leaf blight, can also be debatable for legumes and beans. It is possible to avoid a number of these issues in vegetables by rotating crops, tilling in the autumn, and developing resistant varieties. The next sections explain some issues particular to peas and beans.

Battles For Beans

Here are the most troublesome of this bean issues together with some tips about the best ways best to solve (and stop!) them:

✓ Bald heading: If your bean seedlings emerge in the ground without leaves, then they can have a condition known as bald going. Insects may cause this illness and so can seed that's been damaged. It can happen when you plant the seeds too deep in the ground or from gravel dirt, which causes the leaves to tear off as they attempt to break through the ground. To avoid this illness, prepare the seed bed by removing stones, sticks, and clods of dirt before planting; and do not plant too deep. Leafless beans do not create any plants, so if you find some leafless beans, then pull them out and replant.

✓ Mexican bean beetle: This ladybug comparative has an orange-yellow shell with 16 black spots on it. The adult beetles put masses of lettuce on the undersides of bean plants. If the eggs hatch, the 1/3inch, spiny yellowish young that appear feed onto the bean leaves, defoliating the plant. To control these insects, do the following:

• Plant early maturing types which are completed producing before the bean beetles become abundant.

• Crush any egg whites which you see.

• Clean up old bean plant debris in which the crops overwinter (live during the winter).

• Spray the mature beetles using Pyrethrin (a botanical insecticide made from pyrethrum flowers).

✓ Rust: If your plants have orange or red spots on their leaves before dying when they become yellowish, they might have rust illness. The fungal disease overwinters on bean plant debris left from the garden and infects new plants in summertime once the weather is appropriate (heat temperatures and higher humidity). To stop rust illness, clean up plant debris and until your garden in collapse. The following growing season, rotate bean plantings to a different section of your garden. Also, don't operate on your garden once the leaves are moist; moist leaves offer the moisture which rust disease spores have to have the ability to disperse.

Pesky Pea issues

Peas do not have a lot of pest or disease issues, but here are some to watch out for:

✓ Pea aphid: These 1/8-inch, pear-shaped, green insects suck the juices out of pea leaves and stalks and will stunt a plant's development and make it wilt. If your plants are badly affected with these insects, spray the crops with a safer's insecticidal soap.

✓ Pea enation virus: The pea enation virus is a special difficulty for peas raised in the Pacific Northwest. The virus, which can be spread by aphids (another reason to control the insect), causes the plants' leaves and pods to be deformed and stunted. The optimal solution would be to develop disease-resistant varieties like 'Cascadia'.

HARVESTING YOUR CROP

Since you probably know, in regards to harvesting vegetables, timing is everything. Keep a close watch on your beans and legumes as they begin to grow and select frequently. Beans and peas may become overmatured, tough, and stringy fast, particularly in hot weather. Here is the way to tell if the beans you have planted are prepared for harvest:

✓ You are able to crop snap beans when the pods are crisp and firm and the seeds within are undeveloped. (If the pod is eloquent rather than bumpy, you are aware that the seeds have not raised yet.) Gently hold the beanstalk with one hand and then pull off the beans along with the flip side to prevent breaking up the plants. The more beans you select, the more you are going to receive. That is because the plant wishes to create mature seeds and you keep bothersome it by choosing the pods. So make sure you harvest even when you're not planning to eat all of the beans immediately. Bear in mind, you can always talk about your harvest with starving family and friends.

✓ Harvest shell beans when the pods are complete and green but have not dried out yet. You are able to keep the beans in a fridge for a couple of days prior to cooking them.

✓ Let the bean pods dry on the plant before they inevitably start to divide and then harvest them. Split the bean seeds from the pods by massaging on the pods in your palms, which shatters them. keep the beans in jars in a cool location; you can either eat them or store them to plant the following year. Peas go bad fast, so choosing them if they are under matured instead of overmatured is much better. Additionally, try to cook them the exact same day; they flip starchy quickly in case you keep them for at least 1 or 2 days. Here are some tips for harvesting legumes:

✓ You crop English and skillet once the pods are complete and until they fade in color. Upon harvesting snap peas, cut the cap (stem end) of the pod and choose the string (across the seam) from the pod; all these are the only two portions of the pod which are chewy.

✓ You can select snow peas anytime prior to the pea Seeds in the pods start to form. Following the peas start to fill out, the pods make tough and stringy.

✓ You are able to harvest the tender shoots and tendrils of legumes. Harvest in the conclusion of this shoots back 2 to 3 inches such as the leaves and tendrils. The shoots and tendrils are excellent sautéed or blended raw in salads. It is a means to have the pea taste without the peas and also to use more portions of the pea plant.

Garlic

If any vegetable has undergone a Renaissance recently, it needs to be garlic (Allium sativum). In recent history, garlic has been poo-pooed as a low-class herb which had to be masked in your breath, or you would risk social humiliation. Now it is the posh ingredient in several gourmet foods and touted as a significant medicinal herb to heal everything from earaches to elevated cholesterol. Garlic is also an integral ingredient in certain insect and animal repellents and is extremely capable of repelling vampires (just kidding). These applications come as no real surprise to anybody who understands the background of garlic. It's been used clinically for centuries, but only recently did individuals rediscover its benefits. For some unknown reason, many also think that garlic is challenging to grow. That is not correct. I explain some popular garlic types and describe how to grow garlic in these sections.

Varieties

Though you may grow your own garlic from bulbs purchased in grocery shops, the majority of these varieties are adapted into a California climate. Unless you reside in central California where garlic is mostly commercially developed, it is ideal to pick types from catalogs and neighborhood garden facilities. The beauty of developing your garlic is having the ability to sample the selection of types now available. Deciding upon the number adapted for your area is the very first step, but you can try types from around the world. The tastes of these different types can differ from mild to hot.

Sweet Corn

If all you have ever eaten is candy corn from the supermarket, you are missing out on one of the authentic delights of summer. Fresh-picked, steamed sweet corn has a sweet taste that brings a grin to young and old faces equally. You can also roast corn in an open flame or grill to give it a woodsy taste. By choosing the ideal kinds to grow, you can get sweet corn blossom all summertime. And you do not require a 10-acre area to develop it. Five to six brief rows are all you have to find loads of ears to your loved ones.

Varieties

The kernels of the candy corn plant are actually seeds. Most sweet corn varieties are yellow, white or bicolor (white and yellow blended) kernels. Some heirloom varieties which are mainly utilized for corn flour and roasting include blue and red kernels, which is the point where the red- and - blue-colored corn tortilla chips are derived out of. The color of corn which you pick depends on what flavor you prefer and what kinds grow well where you reside. Varieties older in 65 to 100 days, therefore opt for a sampling which will grow over time in your own garden. Gardeners in cold climates must adhere to quick-maturing types, for example 'Quickie' and 'Early Sunglow'.

The next two newer hybrid types, which maintain their sweetness and tenderness, are commonly found in grocery stores, and their seeds can be found in garden centers and seed standards:

✓ Sugar-enhanced (se) forms possess a particular gene in their cosmetics which raises the sweetness and tenderness of their ears.

✓ Supersweet (sh2) kinds possess a receptor bred to the variety that produces a sweeter than sugar flavor, and they may be kept for a week in the fridge without sacrificing their sweetness. But many believe that what super sweets gain in sweetness, they shed in "actual corn" taste.

Collards

Collards (Brassica oleracea) are an early Cabbage-family harvest that is a stalwart in several Southern gardens. Contrary to cabbages, they do not form heads and will withstand heat and grow well. The entire plant can be eaten at any point, and the big, smooth oval leaves, specifically, taste very good when steamed or blended in soups. Healthwise, they are among the best greens you'll be able to consume; they are high in vitamin A, iron, and calcium. Some good varieties for manufacturing and vitality include 'Champion', 'Georgia', and 'Flash'. Collards like cool weather and grow fast within 60 to 80 days after seeding. Sow seeds directly in the garden 4 to 6 months before the final frost date for a spring crop, and in mid to late summer for a fall crop. Thin the seedlings to ten inches apart. Utilize the thinning in sauces and casseroles.

Okra

Okra (Abelmoschus esculentus) is a southern vegetable which enjoys the warmth. Actually, it's among the few vegetables which keep producing throughout the dog days of summer in the South. This tall (4 to 10 ft), stalky plant generates beautiful, trumpet-like flowers along the primary stem which grow to okra pods, which makes it a gorgeous addition to a flower garden. Some types, like 'Red Burgundy', have vibrant leaves to boot up! Each blossom possibly creates a single pod. The pods could be fried, pickled, boiled, roasted, and eaten by themselves or used in soups and stews like gumbo. Some people do not like the tacky nature of the interiors of the plant, but I really like them grilled using small oil. The conventional okra range is 'Clemson Spineless', which excels in 60 days. However, for anglers using a short growing season, better options "Annie Oakley II' and 'Cajun Delight Hybrid', which adult approximately 50 days from seeding.

"Small Lucy" is a little variety that has burgundy-colored leaves, pods, and stems and just grows 2 feet tall. The yellow flowers have red throats, which makes them a gorgeous contrast to the leaves that are reddish. Due to its dimensions, 'Small Lucy' is a fantastic container plant. Okra needs warmth! Do not direct seed or transplant okra until the soil temperature is at least 65 degrees, usually in the summertime. Start seeds indoors 4 to 6 months ahead of your average last frost date. In cold-winter locations, place black plastic mulch to preheat the dirt and select quick-maturing varieties. Thin plants to 2 feet apart. Fertilize at planting, again if the pods'

shape, then eventually in midsummer with a full organic fertilizer for example 5-5-5.

Peanuts

The peanut is a harvest you can develop that will taste nice and amaze your children (who might have believed that peanuts just grew in ballparks and circuses). The peanut (Arachis hypogaea), a warm-season harvest, is not actually a nut; it is really a legume much like beans and peas. They develop in which okra and sweet potatoes flourish. They enjoy the heat and a long growing season. Nevertheless, even anglers in cold regions may have some success with peanuts, given that they begin early and select short-season varieties like 'Early Spanish'. If you don't develop a field of peanuts, then you likely won't have enough to earn a year's supply of peanut butter but chucked in salt, roasted, or consumed green, fresh peanuts are tasty and healthy snack meals. (I remember when my daughter Elena and I ate nothing but hot, boiled peanuts on a holiday in Georgia one winter.) Various other varieties that have large pods and many more seeds per pod comprise 'Tennessee Red Valencia' and 'Virginia Jumbo'. All of them need 100 to 120 days of hot weather to grow.

Peanuts like well-drained dirt and can tolerate some drought. Plant the seeds with the shells removed, right in the dirt after all risks of frost have passed. Space plants 1 foot apart in rows 2-3 feet apart. The young plant resembles a bush clover plant. Fertilize and water the plants as you would with legumes, but side-dress using 5-5-5 organic fertilizer when blossoms seem to aid with the nut creation. Yellow flowers appear in just 6 months after planting. Hill the plants to kill weeds, mulch with straw, then watch in amazement because the fun part starts.

Radishes

In case you're looking for fast satisfaction, develop radishes (Raphanus sativus). The seeds germinate in times of planting, and many varieties mature their yummy roots in 30 days. Spanish, Daikon, Chinese, and rat-tail radishes take 50 days to grow. When raised in cool weather, radishes are going to have a juicy, slightly hot taste. Obviously, anyone who has raised radishes understands that when radishes are in a situation of too much heat, lack of water, and competition from weeds, you wind up getting a fire-breathing dragon which people usually won't like. I list a few popular varieties and supply strategies for developing radishes in these sections.

Varieties

Most gardeners are knowledgeable about this Spring-planted crimson globes or white cultivated roots located in grocery stores, but exotic-looking foreign radishes are currently showing up in specialty food shops and restaurants. These radishes call for a longer period and are frequently planted to grow in autumn or winter. (They are often referred to as winter radishes for this reason.) Here are a few you can try:

✓ Japanese radishes known as daikons can grow up to 2-foot-long white roots.

✓ Spicy-hot Spanish black radishes seem like round black balls or cylinders and may be held in a root cellar for 6 weeks.

✓ Chinese radishes seem like turnips but are red, green or white on the interior. They taste just like Japanese radishes.

✓ Rat-tail radishes are developed for its spicy-tasting seed pods that shape after flowering.

These kinds work well for the starting gardener:

✓ For your classic white or red round radishes, Try 'Cherriette Hybrid', "Easter Egg II' (a mixture of white and red), and 'Amethyst' (purple skin, white flesh).

✓ For the white or reddish roots, attempt 'French Breakfast' (a mixture of white and red)," White Icicle', or 'D'Avignon' (the very cover of the root is red and the base is white).

✓ For daikons, attempt 'Minowase Summer Cross #3', 'Miyashige', also 'April Cross'.

✓ Some great black Spanish radish types are 'Nero Tondo' (round shape) and 'Long Black Spanish'.

✓ Some Chinese types are 'Red Meat' (green Outside, red inside),'China Rose' (reddish outside and red inside), also 'Misato Green' (green all the way through).

Growing Strategies

The round or elongated "conventional" Radishes are typically planted in early spring up to grow while the temperatures remain cool. Daikons could be planted in spring or summer, depending upon the variety. Black and Chinese radishes, nevertheless, are best planted in late summer or early autumn for a fall or winter crop. Rat-tail radishes are planted in spring. For all sorts of radishes, shape raised beds, fertilize, and sow both in spring and fall. The secret to success with any radish harvest is loosening the dirt nicely, weeding, thinning the plants to provide the roots sufficient space to enlarge (normally 6 inches apart), maintaining the plants well-watered, and developing them when it is cool. It's possible to harvest spring-planted radish roots whenever they begin to form. Harvest daikon, Chinese black radishes if you want them (even though they're most tender when consumed on the side); they could withstand light frosts in the fall. Harvest rat-tail radish pods as soon as they form.

Unusual berries

The fruits we have talked about are the many well-known fruits raised. However, you are also able to find other weird berries and attempt other odd fruits. You can experiment growing a bunch of exotic fruits from all over the world which will grow nicely in your garden. Expand your preference horizons and try some exotic-flavored fruits. At the minimum, they will be a conversation piece! Listed below are a couple of examples:

√ Gooseberries: These woody trees grow 2 to 4 feet tall and broad. They are widely adapted and create red or green, round succulent fruits that are eaten fresh or made into pies and preserves.

√ Currants: These shrubs, that can be a size much like gooseberry bushes, create little red, white, or black berries based on the number. The fruits are juicy and sour, so they are primarily used for preserves, pies, and juices. In reality, currently the juice has been thought to be an elixir that is saturated in health-promoting antioxidants. Like blueberries, these shrubs bear fruit the next year following planting.

√ Dwarf fruit trees: berry plants would be the easiest to grow, Do not shy away from looking for a rainbow cherry or apple tree, also. Tree fruits certainly require more research, but a lot of new types are resistant and dwarf, which makes them ideal additions to a garden. Fruit trees normally produce fruit a couple of years after planting, depending on the kind you are growing.

Other unusual fruits to test based on your experience and climate are figs, citrus, cranberry, elderberry, lingonberry, kiwi, and banana.

CHAPTER 7 - CROP ROTATION, PARTNER SOWING AND SEEDS STARTING

To start seeds inside, all you want is a container, dirt, seeds, moisture, heat, and light. Oh, only if everything in life were so easy. Listed below are the basic steps for planting seeds inside:

1. Sow the seeds in containers full of sterile soil (which garden facilities predict a germinating mix). Keep the seeds in a warm location till germination (if the initial shoots begin to push through the dirt).

2. After the seeds germinate, move the seedlings into some well-lit location (rather under lighting). Though your seedlings are increasing in their well-lit place, make sure to keep them moist.

3. Lean crowded seedlings. If the seedlings' peaks are 3 times the diameter of the kettle, transplant the seedlings to a bigger container.

4. Acclimate the seedlings to outdoor conditions. Adapting your seedlings to the weather states from the fantastic outdoors is known as hardening off.

SOWING YOUR OWN SEEDS

After you have selected the appropriate container and soilless dirt, follow these steps to sow your seeds:

1. Fill the container with moistened growing medium to 1/2 inch of the surface of this container. Soilless mixes are dusty and hard to moist initially. Pour the mixture into a plastic bag, then add enough hot water to moisten the mixture but not twist it to some drippy sand pie. Mix the water and add medium with your palms or a solid wooden spoon, shutting off the start of the bag as far as possible to maintain the dust inside. Remove the dirt in the bag and set it in the container. Gently put down the medium using a flat piece of timber, including a ruler.

2a. If you are planting seeds in a flat, follow along with instructions to sow your seeds: Create shallow furrows (rows) using a blunt rod or by pressing on the narrow edge of a ruler to the medium. Then sow the seeds based on those guidelines:

• Sow small seeds, like carrot, at approximately five to eight seeds per inch, should you would like to transplant them to distinct containers shortly once they develop. Sow bigger seeds, like melons, at a few seeds per inch.

• Sow seeds sparingly, at three to four seeds per inch, if you plan to lean and leave them at precisely the exact same container (instead of transplant into a bigger container). Either way -- transplanting the seeds into a fresh container or leaving them at precisely the exact same container -- works well; it is only a matter of what pots and space you've got. Transplanting into individual pots takes up more space but enables bigger plants such as berries more space for their roots to develop. Smaller crops, like lettuce, develop nicely when thinned and abandoned in their initial containers. It's possible to randomly disperse seeds instead of planting them into row like trenches, but row planting and thinning tend to be simpler.

2b. If You are planting seeds into individual containers, here is the way you sow:

• Place 2 to 4 seeds in each container.

• Afterwards, thin the seedlings, leaving the strongest one.

3. After sowing the seeds at the correct thickness (see the appendix), cover them with nice

grained soil or vermiculite. Label each container or row as most seedlings seem equal. You may buy labels from a nursery or via a mail-order catalog, or you may use old ones out of previously bought nursery transplants. Employing a waterproof pen, record the kind of vegetable, the number, and also the date in which the seed has been planted.

4. Water the seeds lightly with a mister or spray bottle. Keep in mind though that a more powerful flow of water may wash seeds to a single section of this container or transfer them too deeply into the ground.

5. Cover the container with a sheet of clean plastic or a plastic bag to maintain the moisture. If needed, use modest bets to prop up the plastic so that it does not rest along with this ground.

6. Put the planted containers in a hot place. The cooler the temperature, the longer it requires your plants to emerge, so retain them hot and toasty! Some hot spots include the peak of your fridge or near your furnace. But be careful about electric appliances when you water your plants. You are also able to purchase heating mats or cables which keep the soil heated up

from below. Follow the package directions carefully. Never place containers in direct sunlight; the vinyl cover holds in the warmth, cooking your seeds into departure.

7. Verify the containers every day to ensure they are still moist but not wet that they mold. If you notice signs of mold, then loosen the cover and then allow air to get in; the mold must vanish. You can also hook up a little fan to gently blow across the seedlings (minus the plastic cap), maintaining the dirt on the other side. But take care to not wash out the seedlings.

8. Whenever you find the green shoots emerge, remove the plastic cap, and then move your seedlings to a place that offers lots of light along with the appropriate growing conditions for the vegetable. Using 1 /8 refer to the chapter covering that vegetable to get advice concerning the appropriate growing conditions. Until seedlings emerge in the soil, mild is unnecessary, with the exclusion of celery and lettuce seeds. Sow these seeds lightly pressing them in the ground or covering them quite lightly inch of nice soil, then place the containers at a bright place or place them beneath 40-watt incandescent lighting.

SUPPLYING THE PROPER AMOUNT OF LIGHT AND HEAT

The light your young seedlings get is among the most crucial aspects of great development. Putting the seedlings at a south-facing window is one alternative but not necessarily the best one. In a bright window, even plants get just a portion of the light they would acquire outdoors. Windowsill plants frequently become tall and spindly since they make too warm in connection to the light they get. Growing seedlings under fluorescent lighting is a fantastic means to maintain light-hungry plants content. Regular cool-white, 40-watt fluorescent bulbs are all good for starting seedlings. When at all possible, set your lights up near a window so that the plants can get both artificial and natural lighting. The expensive grow lights which you are able to buy in a nursery or via a mail-order seed catalog create the wider spectrum lighting which crops need for flowering and fruiting (even though your seedlings are going to be from the garden until they are prepared to blossom). Regardless of what type of lighting that you have, use one pair of lights (typically two bulbs into a pair) for each 1-foot-width of the seedling-growing region and maintain the bulbs 2 to 4 inches in the tops of the seedlings constantly. Keep the lights on for no longer than 16 hours each day so that the plants can receive their normal rest interval. Inexpensive timers that turn the lights off and on automatically can be found at nurseries and hardware stores.

WATERING YOUR OWN SEEDLINGS

Water your seedlings with care or you risk uprooting them. Mist them using a gentle spray or water from the ground by placing your tank in a bowl of water only long enough for the dirt surface to moist (maintaining them longer than this can harm the plants' roots). After the surface is moist, remove the container from the water and let it drain. Maintain the soil surface gently moist but not soggy. Always water with lukewarm water, also attempt to do this early in the morning, if possible. This way the foliage can dry quickly throughout the day to prevent disease issues. As your plants become more powerful, you can water using a sprinkling can that's a raised, a nozzle which breaks the water to several fine streams. After the crops start growing their initial set of leaves (the leaves to start as the seed germinates are known as seedling leaves, and the following settings are accurate leaves) they possess a larger root system, Allow the soil to dry slightly between watering. Give the plants sufficient water at one time that some of it runs out the drainage holes at the base of the container, but do not leave the container sitting. Overwatering boosts damping-off disorder (see the sidebar "Coping with damping off") and reduces the quantity of air in the soil, causing a weaker root system.

THINNING AND TRANSPLANTING

After seedlings develop their first pair of true leaves (or if onions or leeks, which send a single blade, are two inches tall), you want to narrow them or transfer them out of shallow places to bigger quarters. Thinning is a significant measure, and timing is vital. Should you allow your seedlings to grow overly big in a small container, then their growth is stunted. And if you do not space out them at all, then you end up with weak plants. To thin plants which will keep on growing at exactly the exact same container, then snip out additional seedlings at the soil line using a pair of scissors. If you attempt to pull out these seedlings, you might disturb the roots of those plants which are staying. Also make sure you snip any weak or plants that are stained.

FEEDING YOUR OWN SEEDLINGS

Regular fertilization helps create strong, healthy plants. Some potting soils already have compost blended in, and in some case you do not need to include more. For different forms, use a diluted water-soluble fertilizer to one-third strength (normally one tsp of fertilizer for each gallon of water) to water your seedlings. Water together with the solution once per week.

PARTNER SOWING (COMPANION PLANTING)

A companion plant is one that offers some kind of advantage to other crops growing nearby. It is kind of like how a fantastic friend makes life simpler for you. Plants have great friends, also. These crops are thought to repel certain pests; plant them close to plants where these pests are a frequent issue:

✓ Anise implanted among members of the cabbage family (broccoli, cabbage, cauliflower, kale, etc) is believed to repel imported cabbage worms.

✓ Basil is believed to repel whiteflies, aphids, and spider mites; it is a fantastic companion to tomatoes since these are insects that feed on tomato plants.

✓ Catnip is believed to repel some kinds of aphids, flea beetles, squash bugs, and cucumber beetles.

✓ Garlic can repel nematodes and other soil pests.

✓ Leeks are considered to repel carrot flies.

✓ Marigolds implanted around vegetables are believed to repel root nematodes, Mexican bean beetles, and Colorado potato beetles.

✓ Mustard greens are designed to repel aphids.

✓ Nasturtiums are believed to repel Colorado potato beetles.

✓ Radishes may repel striped cucumber beetles.

✓ Ryegrass may repel root-knot nematodes.

✓ Southernwood may repel moths and flea beetles.

✓ Tansy is designed to repel some aphids, squash bugs, and Colorado potato beetles in addition to ants.

✓ White clover may repel cabbage root flies.

✓ Wormwood may repel flea beetles.

KEEP A PEST-FREE BED BY CROP ROTATION

If you plant the very same vegetables in the same spot every year, you are likely to cause quite a few issues, such as these:

✓ Insects and diseases that invest a part of the life cycle from the soil will construct up there and also be more challenging to control.

✓ Specific nutrients the veggies need will always be depleted and will be more difficult to replace.

CHAPTER 8 - ESSENTIAL TOOLS FOR A VEGETABLE GARDEN

You can probably find most of the things that you need around your home -- particularly if you're working on other outside jobs. Here's a brief list of some helpful gardening equipment:

✓ Gloves allow you to grasp resources better and help you avert hand blisters. Cotton gloves would be the most affordable, but the expensive leather ones -- made of sheep and goatskin, such as -- persist more.

✓ An excellent straw hat with venting retains the sunshine off your skin and allows air to move through and cool your mind.

✓ An excellent pocketknife or set of pruning shears is excellent for cutting edge strings and blossoms.

✓ Sturdy rubber boots, garden clogs, or function boots repel water and supply aid for digging.

✓ Bug repellent and sunscreen keep you comfy and secure while working in the garden.

FREEZING, DRYING, AND CANNING VEGGIES

You can conserve vegetables in three different ways -- by drying, freezing, or canning them to make your crop last more than if you saved your veggies fresh. I don't have enough room to pay for all the details about these different procedures, however, the following list provides you with a thumbnail sketch of each method:

✓ Freezing: This is likely the simplest way to conserve vegetables. But if you would like, simply puree up some berries, place them in a container, and toss them in the freezer and they'll last for 4 weeks. The mixture is very good to use in skillet or soups. Blanching is the practice of dunking the vegetables in boiling water for a moment or 2 and then putting them into ice water to cool them off. You then wash the veggies with a towel and then suspend them in labeled plastic freezer bags.

✓ Drying: This technique could be rather simple, but it has to be performed correctly to avoid spoilage. Essentially, you dehydrate the veggies by placing them out from the sun to dry, by slow baking them in the oven, or using a commercial dehydrator, which you can purchase in most mail-order catalogs (see the appendix). In hot, sunny climates such as California, you can dry 'Roma' tomatoes by slicing them in half and placing them out in sunlight onto a display. Spoilage is an issue, therefore before drying out your veggies, you might have to find some extra info. You usually will need to keep dried veggies in airtight containers; lidded jars work well. You may use dried veggies to create soups and sauces.

✓ Canning: I enjoy the flavor of canned berries the best. Nothing tastes better at the midst of winter. But canning is a fragile and labor-intensive process which could require paring, sterilizing jars, cooking, boiling, and also lots of additional work. I typically put aside an entire weekend can tomatoes and other veggies. I don't wish to dissuade you, but you want some great recipes, some particular gear, and likely some assistance if you would like to can vegetables.

PLACING OFF YOUR VEGETABLES

You have two options when you harvest your plants: eat the veggies straight away, or keep them to use afterward. Particular veggies need different storage requirements to keep their freshness. These states can be outlined as follows:

√ Cold and dry: Temperatures must be between 32 and 40 degrees Fahrenheit, together with 65-percent humidity. You may attain these requirements in many home refrigerators or in a cold basement or garage.

√ Cold and moist: Ideally, your storage space needs to be 32 to 40 degrees Fahrenheit, together with 95-percent humidity. You are able to make these requirements by putting your veggies in refrigerated bags (veggies in luggage without venting are very likely to hamper quicker) and keeping the bags in a fridge.

WATERING HOSES AND CANS

Plants need water to grow, and when mother nature is not cooperating, you want to water frequently. For a huge garden, you might require fancy soaker hoses, sprinklers, and drip irrigation pipes. However, for many small house gardeners, a very simple hose and watering can perform. Rubber hoses are a lesser chance to kink than nylon or plastic pads, but they are normally much heavier to maneuver around. Whatever material you choose, make sure you acquire a hose that is long enough to achieve plants in every area of your garden without needing to take water round the beds to achieve distant plants. Decide on a hose which includes brass fittings and a washer incorporated to the hose; those components make the hose not as likely to fail after prolonged usage. Watering cans can be made from easy, cheap, brightly colored plastic or high end, fancy metal. Vinyl is lighter, but galvanized metal is rustproof and much more appealing. Watering cans come in various sizes, so try several out for relaxation before purchasing. Ensure it is simple to eliminate the sprinkler head, or improved, for cleanup.

Hand Trowels

Hand trowels are crucial for digging in containers, window boxes, and little raised beds. The wider-bladed hand trowels, that can be brightly shaped and round the conclusion, are simpler to use to loosen dirt compared to narrower bladed, V-pointed ones. These thinner blades are better for grinding tough weeds, like dandelions.

HAND CULTIVATORS

A three-pronged hand cultivator is a useful tool to split up dirt clods, straightforward seedbeds, and also operate in granular fertilizer. Additionally, once you plant your little container or elevated bed, the weeds will come if you want it or nota cultivator functions as a fantastic tool to eliminate these youthful weeds as they germinate. When you are digging a planting hole, then a hand cultivator divides the ground more readily compared to a hand trowel. Much like a hand trowel, make certain to opt for a hand cultivator that feels comfortable on your hands which includes a grip firmly fastened to the blade. The steel-bladed kinds will be the most lasting.

Spades and Shovels

Spades and shovels are just two of the most widely used gardening gears. The gap between both is straightforward: A spade is created for grinding, and a shovel was created for scooping and projecting. Shovels traditionally have curved and pointed blades, whereas spades possess flat, right, nearly rotating blades. A fantastic spade is vital in any garden for distributing dirt, manure, or compost. It is crucial for trimming or breaking fresh ground. But many gardeners use spades for whatever from cutting dirt luggage to hammering in bets. Very good spades are rocky. The two spades and shovels arrive in brief - and - long-handled versions. An extended handle gives you more leverage when digging holes, so bear this in mind if you are buying a new spade.

Garden Forks

Useful since a spade is for turning new garden dirt, I find an iron fork is a much better instrument for turning beds which were worked before. The fork slips to the ground as deep as 12 inches, and in precisely the exact same time divides clods and loosens and aerates the soil greater than a shovel. Iron forks look very similar to short-handled spades except they have three to four iron tines in their own heads. The top ones will be those forged from 1 piece of steel with wood grips firmly attached. They are great not just for turning dirt but also for turning compost piles and smelling root crops, like carrots and potatoes.

Garden Rakes

When you dig soil, you have to level it and split dirt clods. An iron rake is an ideal tool for the job though you can use it for this purpose just a few times annually. A 14-inch-diameter, iron-toothed rake ought to have a long, wooden handle that is securely attached to a metallic head. You may turn the metallic head to actually smooth a seedbed level. To get a lightweight but less lasting version of an iron rake, then try out an aluminum rake.

Buckets, Wagons, also Baskets

Even if you do not have a 1,000-square-foot garden, you still should carry seeds, fertilizer, tools, create, and other things around. I enjoy speaking about storage containers since this is where the tools of this trade get very straightforward. Listed below are 3 fundamental containers:

✓ Buckets: For potting soil, fertilizers, and hand tools, a 5-gallon plastic bucket is the best container. You are likely to get one free in the building site: simply be certain that you wash it out nicely. To get a more durable but smaller bucket, then purchase one made out of galvanized steel.

✓ Wagons: For lighter things, like seedlings, use a kid's old red wagon. Wagons are fantastic for transferring plants and tiny bags of compost in your garden, along with the lip to the wagon bed helps maintain these things in place when you have bumpy ground. If you are considering a wagon to maneuver yourself (rather than just gear) around the garden, a new innovation is a saddle using a chair. This sort of wagon generally has a swiveling chair and can be perched on four wheels that are analog, letting you sit down and push yourself throughout the garden as you operate. It has storage space under the chair too.

✓ Baskets: To collect all that fantastic products you develop and harvest, put money into a cable or wicker basket. Wire baskets are easier to use as it is possible to wash the produce while it's still from the basket. Wicker and wooden baskets, even though more durable than steel, are more aesthetically pleasing and trendy in your garden. Piling your products in baskets is much more functional than attempting to balance zucchinis on your arms while taking them out of the garden to your kitchen.

Wheelbarrows and Garden Carts

Invariably you have to move heavy things like dirt and fertilizer from one place to another in your lawn or garden. The two chief choices for transferring stuff that is "bigger than a bread box" are wheelbarrows and garden carts. The simple difference between the two vehicles consists in the wheels. Wheelbarrows have a single wheel along with an oval, alloy tray; garden packs have two wheels and a rectangular wooden tray. Wheelbarrows are maneuverable in tight areas, can flip on a dime, and are simple to dump. A contractor-type wheelbarrow has a deeper box also is well worth the excess investment due to its exceptional quality. To get a lightweight wheelbarrow, try one with a box made from plastic. Garden carts are much better , can carry bigger loads, and are easier to drive than wheelbarrows. A larger-sized garden cart can easily manage loads of dirt, dirt, stone, and bales of hay. Some garden carts have detachable rear panels which make dumping simpler.

Power Tillers

The classic back or front-tined power tiller was developed to aid large-scale anglers save time turning their own gardens in autumn and spring. The huge power tillers (greater than a 5-horsepower motor) are greatest if you have 1,000 square feet or longer to until. Additionally they can be crucial tools for forming raised beds and dividing sod.

MISTAKES YOU NEED TO AVOID

- Raised Bed shouldn't be over four feet broad
- You Strategy for irrigation
- Raised bed garden soil lacks nutrients
- Raised Bed are put near each other
- Pathways Develop weeds and grass
- Neglecting to mulch beds that are raised

ADVICE FOR CULTIVATING AND HARVESTING

Build and Test Your Soil

Start your gardening season with a soil evaluation. This will identify exactly what your dirt lacks or has. Subsequently, you use this info to construct your dirt

Solarize

Utilize solarization to get rid of the growing moderate of soil-borne pests. By dispersing a huge sheet of plastic held in place using bricks, it is possible to grow soil temperatures high enough to destroy weeds, insects and their eggs, and various soil germs. Yes, this necessitates additional time upfront in preparing your possessions, but this method can help save you trouble, time, and expense later in the growing season when you need to take care of infected plants or insects that are damaging.

Utilize Plasticulture

Years ago, farmers used continuous cultivation to remain before weeds, but studies have demonstrated that this can break down the soil structure which you just worked so tough to construct. So use plasticulture, the way where you put black plastic over the ground and plant crops through it. Drip irrigation installed beneath the plastic offers proper moisture. This decreases the demand for dirt farming (weeding) and elevates the soil temperatures at the months when you'd like to expand the season for temperature-sensitive plants.

Plant Cover Crops

"Growing vegetables is extremely taxing on the soil and can strip off its own nutrients. Planting cover crops in the off-season or involving harvest rotations adds back into those very important soil nutrients"

Cover crops include organic matter that is significant, and future plantings gain in the stored nutrients. These plants also enhance soil structure by reducing compaction and opening up dirt pores to keep oxygen and water. A number of the common cover crops include oats, buckwheat, rye, and clover.

Grow With Worms

Worms are excellent little dirt engineers. They split raw organic matter into smaller bits that valuable fungi will make accessible to the plant root system. They also help combine organic matter through the dirt, and their spores enhance soil oxygen and water-holding capacity.

CONCLUSION

Growing our own food is unquestionably among the most helpful pastimes in our lives. We develop food in our garden , crop it and consume it minutes after. Raised together with our own hands, cooked and prepared thickly -- what more can we wish for? Most of us are aware of the health benefits of vegetables. You could even clap your shoulders in cutting air miles. There's surely no petroleum wasted in importing vegetables which come from throughout the world.

When we develop our food, we understand exactly what's gone into developing it. Lots of men and women worry about pesticide residues in food. Even if science demonstrates these pesticide residues from foods are harmless since they're under a particular threshold, a lot of individuals simply prefer to consume food which was raised naturally with no artificial inputs and maybe even raised by themselves. I'm a dedicated organic gardener and I never utilized synthetic fertilizers or synthetic pesticides and that I believe there's not any demand for this. Nature itself takes care of this. As an older gardening buddy said: "Plants only need to grow".

Gardening makes us modest. The food that we grow is raised by Mother Earth and can be given to us as a present. Even after 25 decades of growing veggies I still experience the small wonders of sowing a seed or planting a seed curry and then seeing the revelation.

Until not that long ago, every family needed to produce their own meals. When the plants died, they needed to survive with less and when the plants did well there was a massive sense of satisfaction. There was a powerful sense of purpose in placing food on the table for your family. We no longer possess this feeling of purpose within our Contemporary lives.

Dear Reader

I am an emerging writer and, with the sales made from the book, I can continue my studies to publish other books on the subject. I would appreciate an honest review from you.

Join Kimberley Smith newsletter to be informed about new books:
kimb.smith.books@gmail.com

Thanks for your support

Visit the author's page

Write to: kimb.smith.books@gmail.com

OTHER PUBLICATIONS BY KIMBERLEY SMITH:

Raising Chickens For Eggs:

The Beginner's Guide To Building A Chicken-Coop, To Learn How to Raise A Happy Backyard Flock.
A Homesteading Solution While You Are At Home

Hydroponic Gardening:

A Detailed Guide on Hydronics to Learn the Principles Behind Gardening and Build a Wonderful System While at Home. Techniques for Your Vegetable Cultivations

Printed in Great Britain
by Amazon